Presencing

Presencing

7 Practices for Transforming Self, Society, and Business

C. OTTO SCHARMER
KATRIN KAUFER

BK

Berrett–Koehler Publishers, Inc.

Berrett-Koehler Publishers, Inc.
1333 Broadway, Suite P100
Oakland, CA 94612–1921
Tel: (510) 817–2277   Fax: (510) 817–2278   bkconnection.com

ORDERING INFORMATION
Quantity sales. Special discounts are available on quantity purchases by corporations, associations, and others. For details, please go to bkconnection.com to see our bulk discounts or contact bookorders@bkpub.com for more information.
Individual sales. Berrett-Koehler publications are available through most bookstores. They can also be ordered directly from Berrett-Koehler: Tel: (800) 929–2929; Fax: (802) 864–7626; bkconnection.com.
Orders for college textbook / course adoption use. Please contact Berrett-Koehler: Tel: (800) 929–2929; Fax: (802) 864–7626.

Distributed to the US trade and internationally by Penguin Random House Publisher Services.

The authorized representative in the EU for product safety and compliance is EU Compliance Partner, Pärnu mnt. 139b-14, 11317 Tallinn, Estonia, www.eucompliancepartner.com, +372 5368 65 02.

Berrett-Koehler and the BK logo are registered trademarks of Berrett-Koehler Publishers, Inc.

Printed in The United States of America

Berrett-Koehler books are printed on long-lasting acid-free paper. When it is available, we choose paper that has been manufactured by environmentally responsible processes. These may include using trees grown in sustainable forests, incorporating recycled paper, minimizing chlorine in bleaching, or recycling the energy produced at the paper mill.

Library of Congress Cataloging-in-Publication Data

Names: Scharmer, Claus Otto, 1961– author. | Kaufer, Katrin, author.
Title: Presencing : 7 practices for transforming self, society, and business / C. Otto Scharmer, Katrin Kaufer.
Description: First edition. | Oakland, CA : Berrett-Koehler Publishers, [2025] | Includes bibliographical references and index.
Identifiers: LCCN 2024044548 (print) | LCCN 2024044549 (ebook) | ISBN 9798890570284 (paperback ; alk. paper) | ISBN 9798890570291 (pdf) | ISBN 9798890570307 (epub)
Subjects: LCSH: Social change. | Organizational change. | Change (Psychology)
Classification: LCC HM831 .S3559 2025 (print) | LCC HM831 (ebook) | DDC 303.4—dc23/eng/20250116
LC record available at https://lccn.loc.gov/2024044548
LC ebook record available at https://lccn.loc.gov/2024044549

First Edition
33 32 31 30 29 28 27 26 25   10 9 8 7 6 5 4 3 2 1

Book production: Westchester Publishing Services
Cover Design: Olaf Baldini
Cover and Interior Illustration: Olaf Baldini

To the awakening of our dormant superpower:
The power to align attention, intention, and agency,
individually and collectively.

Contents

Introduction

In this time of accelerated breakdown and disruption, the capacity we need most is our capacity to sense and actualize the highest future possibility—the future "that stays in need of us" to manifest.[1] That is what we call *presencing,* and that is what this book is about.

Together with our colleagues we first articulated this idea in two books published about twenty years ago.[2] Since then two things have changed: First, the urgency with which we need to cultivate and enhance our capacity for deep transformation and presencing the emerging future has increased dramatically; and second, the practical methods and tools for accessing this deep human capacity, both as individuals and collectively, have been significantly improved.

This book has been written for everyone who shares this *felt sense* of a *possible future* that is different from what is happening around us now—a future that, to use Martin Buber's words, "stays in need of *us* to come into reality as *it* desires."[3] It builds on our experience of working with citizens, changemakers, leaders, organizations, and communities aiming to address the polycrisis facing our planet. While we have seen an accelerating crisis across the planet, we also see a growing movement of deep transition and profound change, a new landscape of innovators, initiatives, and communities that are, in the face of our mounting challenges and disruptions, co-pioneering novel and regenerative ways of living and working together. The purpose of this book is to support and inspire this incipient planetary movement and all its current and potential future members—that is, all of us who want to co-shape a better future.

If you are

- a person who wants to create practical results, you can use this book as a guide to upgrade your "toolkit" of sensemaking and co-creation as you work on deep transition and systems change;
- someone who is aspiring to bring something new into the world, you will find many stories of inspirational change that are currently unfolding across the planet; or
- a person who has mixed feelings about the current situation, senses that collectively we are moving in the wrong direction, and wonders how you might be part of a different story of the future but don't have a clue what that might look like or how it can happen, this book may be perfect for you because it will take you on a journey of deep sensemaking and will help you to manifest your highest future possibilities.

The purpose of this book is to strengthen your capacity to sense, connect with, and actualize your highest future potential through presencing. The word *presencing* is a combination of two words: *presence* and *sensing*. It describes the moment when we connect with and act from a future potential that depends on us to bring it into the now.

The seven chapters of this book introduce seven core concepts and ideas, which we outline here.

1. Are We Sinking or Are We Going to Rise?

We begin by differentiating between two narratives that are shaping our current moment. One is a story we all know very well: the story of destruction (of planet, of people, of ourselves). It's a story that is amplified by the trillion-dollar social media industry every moment of every day. The other story is less known and is not amplified by any comparable mechanism. It is a story of regeneration, healing, and deep personal and systemic transition. It's the most significant, least well-told story of our time.

2. From Social Systems to Social Fields

The second idea that shapes this book is the concept of the social field, which was strongly influenced by Otto's experience growing up on a farm in northern Germany.

> Every Sunday our family walked across the land, where my father taught us that the quality and yield of our annual harvest depended on the quality of the soil. Plants visible above the soil depend on the nutrition and conditions of the soil they are rooted in.

A *social field* has a *visible* part aboveground (the tangible part of the system) and an *invisible* part below the surface: the *social soil*—that is, the qualities of awareness and relationships that people in a system operate from.

The concept of the social field builds on the profound work of systems thinking over many decades and seeks to further evolve it to reckon with the complexities of the twenty-first century. The concept of social fields expands systems thinking by grounding it in the *sources* of attention, intention, and agency—that is, the quality of the social soil.

What *soil* is for the biosphere—a connector, enabler, and regulator— *attention* is for the social sphere.

Soil, organic matter, is a living sphere that consists of billions of microorganisms, connecting the atmosphere with the lithosphere and functioning as the medium through which these spheres interact through processes like climate regulation, water retention, and nutrient cycling. Healthy soil is essential for the *biosphere* to flourish.

Likewise, attention connects the tangible, visible side of social systems (actions and words) with the intangible, invisible side of them (thoughts and feelings) and functions as the medium through which these two realms interact through processes such as empathic listening, dialogue, teamwork, and social well-being. Shared attention is essential to allowing the entire *social sphere* to flourish.

When farmers cultivate their fields, they need practical tools to do so. What the chisel plow does to cultivate the agricultural soil, the seven practices presented in this book do to cultivate the social soil.

There is a functional equivalence between *turning* and *opening* the *soil* to improve its fertility (the cultivation work of the farmer) and *turning* and *opening* our *attention* to improve the quality of the social soil—the cultivating work that all of us do, whether we are educators in the classroom, leaders in companies or pioneers among their stakeholders, nurses and doctors in their teams and with their patients, parents with their loved ones, or scientists and inventors in their labs.

The seven practices all work by *bending the beam of attention* back onto its source. The moment we start to pay attention to our attention we begin to become aware, i.e., we begin to turn the camera back onto ourselves—that's when the real cultivation of the *social soil* begins.

3. The Wheel of Deep Change: Looking into the Systems Mirror

The third concept introduced in this book, the "Wheel of Deep Change," builds on the idea of the social soil and applies it to our current societal polycrisis and how we can transform it. The upper hemisphere of the Wheel depicts the tangible side of our societal sectors, including agriculture, education, health, business, finance, technology, and governance (see Color Plate 4).

The lower hemisphere depicts the *social soil* side of these systems, or their operating systems, and how we can cultivate it through the seven core practices of eco-system leadership to enable transformation.

The Wheel functions as a *whole systems mirror* for depicting, diagnosing, and dialoguing about our current evolutionary moment. Through this mirror we can see three major spheres of change (or deep change) that cut across the upper and lower hemisphere: the outer sphere (2.0: output efficiency-centric), the middle sphere (3.0: user- and stakeholder-centric), and the inner sphere or deep change (4.0: eco-system and regeneration-centric). A looming sphere of 1.0 regression or revival around the edges (input and control-centric) makes up the fourth sphere.

These four spheres of change—from shallow to deep—map a comprehensive landscape of systems transformation in ways that allow us to identify, track, and reflect our own systems from multiple angles and locate them in the evolutionary context of the whole (see Foldout Color Plate 1).

4. Presencing, Absencing, and Fourth-Person Knowing

The fourth core concept that grounds this book is presencing. Presencing is about meeting the emerging future in the moment. Where can we find practical anchors for that type of deepened acting, being, and knowing?

In our applied work on systems change, we have found that most initiatives for deep transition do not deliver on their intention unless they are able to access a deeper source of knowing within their eco-system. We call this "fourth-person knowing."[4] Fourth-person knowing is different from the three traditional types of knowing that form the foundation of today's sciences, social sciences, and learning. These are

first-person knowledge: subjective (how I feel or experience something)
second-person knowledge: intersubjective (what we can share and agree on)
third-person knowledge: objective (what we can count, measure, or record)

fourth-person knowledge: what emerges around the edges of the other three forms of knowledge, blending with but also transcending them. It is trans-subjective in that it is very personal but emerges *through you* rather than being *of* you and it gives us access to a deeper form of self-knowing, of who we really are, and what it is that we are here for.

We can access this deeper, fourth-person way of knowing by presencing. Presencing is about sensing and actualizing the future that wants to emerge through us *in the now*. It is a deepened level of knowing in which something is *looking at* you because it *depends on you* to manifest.

Fourth-person knowing is neither extraordinary nor new. It is not extraordinary because it is a widely distributed experience that many of us have had glimpses of, often without ever becoming fully aware of it. And it is not new in the sense that for many generations, pioneers or people who have created and brought something new into being have had experiences of it. What *is* perhaps new is that in our current time, this experience, which makes us aware of our need to connect with a future that depends on us, is a lot more common.

The concept of fourth-person knowing is part of a larger shift in consciousness that will be discussed in chapter 4. Without it, we will only end up doing more of the same. The great Nigerian philosopher and poet Báyò Akómoláfé describes our current way of operating as *running in circles*.[5] Running in circles is a type of behavior that he compares with ant mills, in which army ants chase each other in a circle, endlessly, until they finally die of exhaustion. It's a commentary on a collective behavior that illuminates why we are in need of profound change.

5. Eco-system Leadership: Seven Practices for Cultivating the Social Soil

The fifth core concept concerns eco-system leadership. Eco-system leadership is the capacity to align attention, intention, and agency at the level of the whole. It is grounded in these seven core practices that are outlined in chapter 5 and form the backbone of this book:

becoming aware: bending the beam of attention back onto ourselves

listening: holding the space within; listening with your mind and heart wide open

dialogue: holding spaces for systems to see and sense themselves

presencing: holding the space for meeting the future in the now

emerging: holding spaces for crystallizing the future that we want to create

co-creating: holding spaces for exploring the future by doing

eco-system governance: holding spaces for coordinating around shared intention

These practices enable us to break old habitual patterns of operating. The practices are accompanied by the U-process. At its core the U-process outlines a pathway—individual and collective—of *opening* up, *decentering*, and operating from emerging future possibilities. In other words, the U-process enables individuals, groups, and societies to operate from the future potential that needs *us* in order to come into being.

6. The Future Is Already Here: Three Transformations

The sixth core concept that grounds this book is that the future is already here. The transformational shifts of our core systems have already been prototyped in many places. They can be summarized as

- shifting our economies from ego to eco: from silos to systems awareness;
- shifting democracies from gridlock to formats that are more dialogic, distributed, and direct; and
- shifting lifelong learning from transactional to transformative inspired by fourth-person knowing.

We describe how these transformations can also serve as a pathway for positive peace in a world that has seen a sharp increase in the use of violence. Creating peace through peaceful means is, as we learned from our professor

Johan Galtung, the founder of peace research as a science, grounded in the capacity to address the root issues of all forms of violence—direct, structural, and cultural—to which we would also add a fourth: *attentional violence*, not seeing others in terms of who they really are, from which all other forms of violence tend to arise.[6]

7. Protect the Flame

The seventh core concept is personal: What is ours, *what is mine to do?* What does it take to protect the "flame"—that is, to cultivate the connections to the sources of our own essence and potential? What does it take to unlock our dormant superpowers related to the seven practices? It takes transformational learning infrastructures. It takes new and scalable digital, social, and physical support structures that help the emerging movement that we are witnessing across the planet to connect to its deeper sources of knowing. These infrastructures revolve around strengthening three connections:

the downward connection: to the land, to the power of place, that we can feel in our embodied structures, individually and collectively

the horizontal connection: to those surrounding us in our eco-system context that we co-hold and co-evolve with

the upward connection: to the highest future potential that depends on us to manifest

How do we create "islands of coherence" that have the capacity to shift the larger system when it is far from balance? By embodying and integrating these three primary connections. What is the smallest unit for these islands of coherence? YOU. It's us. It's our capacity to align attention, intention, and agency. It's through these practices, described throughout this book, that we strengthen our capacity to meet the moment through presence.

Ultimately, no one can do this alone. We can only do this together. Which is why all the seed initiatives and small *islands of coherence* that we see popping up around and among us need to be connected and cultivated toward eco-systems of healing and regeneration.

But the foundation of all of this is clearly in our control: it involves cultivating the social soil by deploying the *seven practices* featured in this book to realigning *attention, intention,* and *agency.* The more we do and embody this, the more we grow in the direction of the awareness that we hold.

Enjoy the read!

Chapter 1

Are We Sinking or Are We Going to Rise?

When a system is far from equilibrium,
small islands of coherence in a sea of chaos have the capacity
to elevate the entire system to a higher order.
—ILYA PRIGOGINE

We live in a time of deep transition that in hindsight will be seen as a threshold moment in the history of our planet: a moment when *how* we showed up—as individuals, as groups, as organizations, or as systems—began to refocus and reshape our pathways forward.

Within a few centuries, our descendants will likely look back and say, "Yes, those were the years when the old systems of extraction and ego began to crash and burn and something new started to take shape." At first, these seeds of the new went unnoticed, but then they began to show up as *small islands of coherence,* just as plants are invisible to the eye until right before their shoots pierce the soil. Yet the miracle of germination is already well underway *before* these sprouts meet the light of day.

Two Narratives

That is the moment we are living in now. The old structures of extraction are still here, clashing, crashing, burning, and sometimes resurfacing even more strongly than before (for a period); at the same time a new *awareness* of the whole, a new way of *relating* and connecting with each other, with the planet, and with ourselves is beginning to take shape. It's an awareness that is deeply rooted in a diverse array of wisdom traditions, yet it is evolving in response to our planetary challenges, essentially shifting our way of operating from *ego* to *eco*, from *doubt, hate*, and *fear* to *curiosity, compassion*, and *courage*.

That subtle and mostly unnoticed awakening *awareness of the whole* is a story that even the carriers of these seeds—the many of us—are only partially aware of. Here is a symptomatic data point. According to the 2023–2024 UN Human Development Report, 69 percent of people around the world would be willing to sacrifice part of their income to contribute to climate change mitigation, while only 43 percent believe that others would do the same.[1] In other words, more than two out of three people on the planet are willing to sacrifice some portion of their personal well-being to address climate change. This movement in the making has the potential to emerge as the biggest the planet has ever seen—yet most people don't believe that others share that kind of commitment. This misperception gap is a barrier that prevents collective action from happening in more intentional and powerful ways. But it presents a fascinating puzzle: How to make this potentially widespread movement *see itself*?

This gradual awakening of a new awareness matters because a movement that is not aware of itself is *not* a historic force. And yet it's a movement that in many ways already exists all over the planet.

It's a movement, or unmovement, with *a thousand faces*, often transcending the traditional forms of protest against what's broken. It's an (un-)movement that cuts across sectors, classes, ideologies, and identities. It manifests through an *extended awareness*—an awareness that emerges when we *bend the beam of observation back* onto ourselves, causing us to see ourselves through the eyes of others—our partners, friends, stakeholders, and even our enemies—or through the eyes of future generations.

Bending the Beam of Attention

One moment in the late twentieth century that captured a shift in our collective consciousness was when the astronauts of *Apollo 8* were the first to leave the gravitational field of our planet and see it from outer space. The iconic *Earthrise* photograph was taken by astronaut William Anders on December 24, 1968. It depicts the rise of our beautiful home planet over the lifeless moonscape, and it altered human consciousness. It changed the trajectory of our gaze: instead of looking for something *out there* (the surface of the moon), it bent the beam of attention *back onto ourselves.* Anyone who experiences a similar attentional turn—seeing themselves through the eyes of those who surround them—comes away with a different (and often somewhat altered) state of awareness. Our twenty-first-century world provides us with plenty of possibilities to leave our own "center of gravity" (the ego view) and to look at a situation through the eyes of different stakeholders (the eco view). For example, the climate crisis requires us to look at every action we take, not only from an individual but also from a global perspective, and from the viewpoint of future generations.

This planetary awareness has many historic lineages and origins. These include the liberation movements in the Global South inspired by Mahatma Gandhi and grounded in nonviolence (*ahimsa*) and truth (*satyagraha*); the Civil Rights Movement in the United States, which changed the country and inspired the world; the anti-Apartheid movement in South Africa and civil rights movements in other regions; the women's movements; manifold movements for environmental, social, and racial justice; the various peace movements; the movements for Indigenous people's rights; and the various movements devoted to inner development and mindfulness.

These movements for transformative change remain inspiring, but they have also generated a backlash against civil society and a resurgence of populist movements or sentiments across many places and regions.

The backlash tends to show up in places of neglect, where people don't feel seen, respected, valued for who they are, or helped when something is taken from them, whether it has to do with their work, their possessions, or their sense of security—essentially wherever people are not treated with dignity.

The 2023–2024 UN Human Development Report highlights a growing agency gap. Half of the people surveyed worldwide report that they have limited or no control over their lives, and more than two-thirds perceive that they have no agency in the collective decision-making of their countries; they feel that their voice does not count.[2]

These worrying developments are co-shaped and amplified by a social media machine whose algorithms prioritize hate speech and misinformation over facts and real dialogue. Therefore, three foundations of our societies are being weakened and undermined: democracy (through mass polarization), factual information or truth (through mass misinformation), and human well-being (through mass depression: the pandemic of mental health).

Islands of Coherence

Given this context, the forces of disruption—including climate destabilization, inequality, and artificial intelligence (AI)—and the felt loss of agency, we have found that the concept of *islands of coherence* can help us to refocus on where the real opportunity is—in *our very own agency*—that is, in our capacity to act.

"When a system is far from equilibrium, small islands of coherence in a sea of chaos have the capacity to elevate the entire system to a higher order." Those words, attributed to chemist and Nobel laureate Ilya Prigogine (1917–2003), articulate the idea of bifurcation points. Bifurcation points are critical points in nonlinear systems where small changes in one place (or one variable) can affect how the whole system behaves. Many people sense that we are living in such a moment, that we are at a crossroads, where the future of the planet hangs in the balance.

What is the smallest unit of an *island of coherence?* It's you, it's me, it's each of us: it's in our quality of attention, it's in our quality of relationships.

Islands of coherence redirect our attention back to our own *agency*, to what *we* can do. They help us to realign our attention, intention, and agency within the small microcosms of the systems we operate in.

Diverging Forces

In our current moment, many of us find ourselves pulled *forward* and *backward* at the same time: dragged backward toward old structures and ways of operating ("again") and pulled forward into emerging new opportunities and ways of operating that, in our better moments, we can connect with by *leaning in* with our minds and hearts wide open. Those places of possibility depend on *us* to bring them into being. As the tension between being pushed backward and pulled forward begins to intensify, we notice several interesting shifts.

Outside of us, we see increasing levels of breakdown and the increasing collapse of old structures, institutions, and behaviors that have long outlived their usefulness. We see people putting up walls—the rise of divisions, polarization, and echo chambers that throw us into separation and loneliness. But we also see walls coming *down*—the emergence of deepened connections, of people joining forces to create new ways to live and work together.

Moreover, we can notice a new awareness of *ourselves* and our own levels of agency. *How* we pay attention matters. The *intentions* we hold make a profound difference. The aligning of *attention*, *intention*, and *agency* is perhaps the most powerful force for transformation present on this planet now. The quality of our *presence* makes *all* the difference to us, to others, and to our planet.

Finally, there is only one pathway for truly connecting with our highest future potential: the journey of the *heart*. The journey of the heart is the gateway to *presencing*. The heart becomes an organ of perception that enables the innate human ability *to sense and actualize* our highest future potential—a future that is *looking at us* because it cannot manifest without us. Presencing can be thought of as a blend of words: *presence* (embodying and acting from the presence of the future now) and *sensing* (feeling a future potential). It is the practice of meeting the emerging future in the present moment.

We Collectively Create Results That Nobody Wants

Two profound developments set the stage for the decades ahead. The first is a massive intensification of *disruption*, *distraction*, and *disorientation* that has led to the polycrisis facing civilization and our planet. These *disruptions* feed the well-known divides of our time:

the ecological divide: a disconnect between Self and Nature that manifests in climate destabilization and massive biodiversity loss

the social divide: a disconnect between Self and Other that manifests in inequality, hyperpolarization, violence, and war

the spiritual divide: a disconnect between self and Self, between who I am now and who I could be. This divide manifests as a pandemic of mental health issues including anxiety, hopelessness, loneliness, and depression.

The *distraction* and *disorientation* are amplified by a social media–based industry that thrives on diverting and hijacking our attention. In the context of our twenty-first-century attention economy, our ability to pay attention, to focus, is the ultimate scarce resource. The business model of social media runs on amplifying the noise (the more extreme your viewpoint, the more amplification you get through algorithms—i.e., the louder your megaphone is), to distract our attention (toward paid content), and to manipulate our behavior (which is the basis for a trillion-dollar industry that keeps pumping noise into our systems).

We collectively create results that no one wants. Almost no one gets up in the morning, looks in the mirror, and says, "All right, I'm looking forward to spending another day inflicting harm and violence on nature, on others, and on myself." Yet collectively, that's exactly what we keep doing. Generally, we know what the problems are. We also often know what the solutions are. But we are not implementing these solutions collectively in ways that will transcend our collective knowing-doing gap.

Recognizing that gap adds to a felt sense for many that *perhaps it's already too late* to have any meaningful influence on how the future evolves. According to the 2023–2024 UN Human Development Report, 50 percent of us believe that we have lost agency in our personal lives, and 68 percent of us believe we have no voice in collective decision-making.[3]

The Condition of Collective Depression

Even though the felt sense of hopelessness and the collective condition of depression are widespread, our moment of agency has not passed by any stretch of the imagination.

Recently, Otto worked with a group of UN leaders from various agencies. While preparing to launch a workshop series on a future UN (UN 2.0) that better meets the moment we are living in, the group was feeling weighed down by the recent turn of events in the Middle East and other crises around the globe. At that moment our Zambian Presencing Institute colleague Martin Kalungu-Banda shared his own motivation for joining our effort and asked: "What if everything we are experiencing now *is exactly the moment the UN was created for?*"

> Stillness. As this question landed on each of us, I felt a new energy begin to emerge in the room. **"What if,"** someone else asked shortly after, **"everything that we are experiencing right now is exactly the moment that we—as a community of leaders and changemakers—were born for?"** Suddenly the blanket of collective depression that had been weighing on us was lifted. The challenges had not gone away, but we now saw our current reality from a *different* vantage point: a place of possibility connected with our own path of agency—regardless how small that agency may be. That shift changes everything. It focuses our attention on what is ours to do.

In many ways that story is prototypical of our current moment. If you take in all the data and trends, you tend to get depressed. But how can we stay informed and avoid depression and a sense of futility? That's why Martin's question is so helpful. **What if everything that we are experiencing right now is exactly the moment that we were born for? What if everything that *I* am experiencing right now is exactly the moment that *I* was born for?** What if now is exactly the moment for us to wake up—to *bend the beam of attention back onto ourselves* and to see our current situation from a viewpoint of possibility and emerging potential? This perspective relocates the source of our attention in an *awareness* of a deepened relationship with our *planet*, with *each other*, and with *ourselves*.

Here is another data point worth considering. According to a 2021 poll, *three out of four* people in the G20 countries support the transformation of our economic systems to better address climate change and social inequality (G20 countries represent 60 percent of the world's population and 80 percent of global GDP).[4] Three-quarters of those surveyed support transformative change, and, as noted above, two out of three people are willing to sacrifice some part of their income to address the climate challenge. Yet, most of us also underestimate how many others share these views.

The Pando Forest

Think of this "perception gap" like this: there's a huge forest covering a massive landscape, but most members of that forest (the individual trees) are only aware of a small portion of the surrounding trees; they are unaware of the size and interconnectedness of the whole forest.

Consider the example of the so-called Pando tree in the state of Utah in the United States. The Pando is an extraordinary natural phenomenon consisting of a grove of aspens covering roughly 106 acres. It is estimated that the Pando could be up to eighty thousand years old. Its trees are all interconnected through a single root system, making it one of the largest and oldest living organisms on Earth. Each tree in the grove is genetically identical, effectively making the entire forest a single living entity.

The planetary movement in the making has some striking parallels with the Pando phenomenon. What's most important—the interconnected root system—is virtually invisible. In movements for social and systems change around the world, we are beginning to see similar "root connections" on many levels of *interconnectedness* or "interbeing" (as the great Zen teacher Thích Nhất Hạnh describes it).[5] In many places these connections are appearing organically, even though the seeds are still dormant and invisible to the eye.

Shifting Consciousness by Making Systems
See and Sense Themselves

Over the years, we have learned that experiencing oneself as part of a community of inspired changemakers can profoundly deepen and activate one's personal intention and agency.

Every year since 2015 we have organized a yearlong free program called *u-lab: Leading from the Emerging Future*. The u-lab is an online–offline course that gives changemakers free access to tools and methods for bringing about transformative change.[6] Since 2015, over 260,000 u-lab participants from 194 countries have created thousands of local in-person "hubs" to help each other devise solutions to their local challenges. Many of these hubs generate ideas and initiatives year after year. It's like a different kind of Pando in the making: a planetary field of connections that keep co-generating countless shoots across the entire eco-system.

In an environment saturated with online offerings, why does a course like u-lab continue to activate the powerful experiences of deep, lasting relationships and an ongoing stream of initiatives? Much of it has to do with the Pando-like structure of the roots and the soil that the u-lab generates. The u-lab "live sessions" are broadcast from a small classroom at MIT to the entire community as a way of "holding" a shared space for all the participants. In these sessions we invite participants into moments of *intentional stillness*, of sensing what emerges from the felt presence of the global community.

We have learned from many participants that being a part of a planetary social field has a significant empowering impact on their local initiatives. They tell us that these are the moments when they feel a part of a global field of connection, being part of a bigger story that deeply resonates with their own deepest intention, a story of pioneering pathways for co-shaping the future through shifting the social fields in their own local contexts wherever they are.

These repeated patterns—with roughly one-third of u-lab participants reporting about life-changing experiences—makes us ask the following questions: How might we further democratize access to such spaces, methods, and tools? What would it take for everyone who has an interest to explore and experience the Pando-style root connections that we all share across sectors, systems, and cultural boundaries? What would it take to bring this hybrid of capacity building, eco-system activation, and planetary movement building to the next level?

We know that to change systems we need to create spaces that allow everyone involved to sense and see themselves as part of the larger whole. In other words, to transform a system we must transform the consciousness (the mindsets) of those who co-enact that system moment to moment. And to do that we need to create new forms and qualities of holding spaces that allow the system to *see and sense itself.*

Recent large historic transformations, such as decolonization, the collapse of the Berlin Wall, or the end of Apartheid in South Africa, are not the result of sudden changes or decisions. They require intentional support structures and hard work over many years, decades, and often generations.

But all historic shifts begin with individuals who take the first steps—steps that at first seem very small. These shifts begin when small groups, small islands of coherence with the right support structure, grow over time to become *eco-systems of coherence.* Building islands of coherence begins when we *bend the beam of attention back onto its source,* when we become aware of our relationships with others, with our planet, and with our Selves.

Holding the Gaze Steady: Aligning Attention and Intention

If a shift toward forming islands of coherence and from there to an awareness of the larger system is part of the journey of change, where do we start? We believe that the most practical and powerful starting point is *realigning attention and intention*—in other words, bringing intention into our social interactions and relationships. The journey through this book and the tools at the end of each chapter are designed to help you in that process.

Traditional mindfulness and awareness practices use breathing, sensations in the body, or perhaps a mantra (a word, sound, or phrase) to focus our attention. Every practitioner develops the practice that works best for them. You may already have yours.

In this book we suggest practices that offer related but different ways to contemplate the current moment. By *holding our gaze steady* on this object of contemplation and inquiry we engage in a structured process of *bending our beam of attention back* onto its source—*ourselves*—and onto what emerges through it.

Chapter 2

From Social Systems to Social Fields

Otto's parents converted their family farm from conventional to re-generative agricultural practices in the mid- to late 1950s.

One of the things I learned from them is that a regenerative farm-er's focus must *always* be on *improving the quality of the soil.* About almost twenty years ago, I took that lesson as inspiration and wrote the book *Theory U,* which introduced and deepened the concepts of awareness-based systems change and *presencing,* or *learning from the future as it emerges.*[1]

That book began with a description of our old family farm in northern Germany where, every Sunday morning, my parents would take me and my siblings on a walk across the fields. Every now and then my father would stop, bend down, and with his hand scoop up some of the soil and examine it. What I learned on these walks is that the *living soil is* the farmer's most significant teacher.

That's what I hoped to do with *Theory U*—invite the reader on a field walk across the *social fields* of our time. Throughout that book, every now and then we'd stop, bend down, and pick up a piece of data—a story, an experience, an observation—in order to listen to and learn from the changemaker and social scientist's most significant teacher: the *social field*.

What has become clearer to us since then is that the role *soil* plays in the biosphere is comparable to the role that *attention* plays in our social worlds. In both, a mediation between two spheres or domains of existence gives rise to a new world.

Soil mediates between and connects the atmosphere aboveground and what is beneath it, the lithosphere, in ways that provide climate regulation, water retention, and nutrient cycling. As organic matter, soil is essential for planetary flourishing.

Attention also mediates between and connects two distinct spheres: the visible part of social systems (actions, words, tangible results) and the invisible part (the qualities of relationships or awareness), in ways that provide empathic listening, deep dialogue, collaborative teamwork, and shared systems awareness. Attention, together with empathy and intention, is essential for human and social flourishing.

When farmers cultivate their fields, they need practical tools. What the chisel plow does for cultivating the agricultural field, the seven practices introduced in this book do for the cultivation of the social field. There is some functional equivalence between *turning the soil onto itself* (the cultivation work of the farmer) and *turning our attention onto itself*, which is what we call reflection or contemplation and is the backbone of all advanced work in leadership, education, healing, and systems change.

Systems Thinking and the Iceberg Model

One foundation of our work as action researchers and changemakers is the concept of systems thinking, along with its methods and tools. Starting in the early twentieth century, general systems theory and, a bit later, systems thinking both used the *iceberg* as a metaphor for visualizing the distinction between the visible symptoms of a problem (the 10 percent of the iceberg visible above the waterline) and the invisible roots of a problem (the 90 percent of the iceberg below the waterline). The point of the metaphor is that leading change in any kind of system requires more than reacting against the symptoms (the 10 percent at the top); leaders also need to understand and address the deeper root problems at play.

One of the first widely known applications of systems thinking to environmental challenges was *The Limits to Growth*, published in 1972 for the Club of Rome.[2] It warned of global ecological and economic collapse if current growth trends continued and emphasized the need for sustainable development practices.

Today, more than fifty years on, that message is just as urgent. In a recent report of the Transformational Economics Commission, led by the Club of Rome, which Otto has been a part of, the main focus was on five intertwined root issues that call for five related turnarounds:[3] eliminate poverty, reduce inequality, empower women, transform food systems, and turn around energy systems (visit earth4all.life/). To be transformative, however, these five turnarounds will require a sixth: a shift in consciousness. This is what presencing, Theory U, and the Inner Development Goals (IDGs) are about, which we have helped co-create as part of a global movement. The IDGs complement the SDGs (Sustainable Development Goals) by emphasizing the interior dimension, as outline in a recent paper.[4]

The "extended iceberg model" in Figure 2.1 depicts the symptoms of each crisis above the waterline and their underlying root issues below the waterline: structures (processes, policies, procedures), paradigms of thought (how we frame an issue), and consciousness or the deeper sources from which we operate (creativity, purpose, and self).[5]

In our two-plus decades of experience facilitating change initiatives spanning sectors and geographies, we have repeatedly recognized three key learning experiences.

First, when we continue to create collective results that no one wants, any solution requires us to not just do "more of the same." Our planetary polycrisis finds us looking into an ecological, social, and spiritual abyss. Collectively, we are burning more fossil fuel, keep killing people in unwinnable wars, and

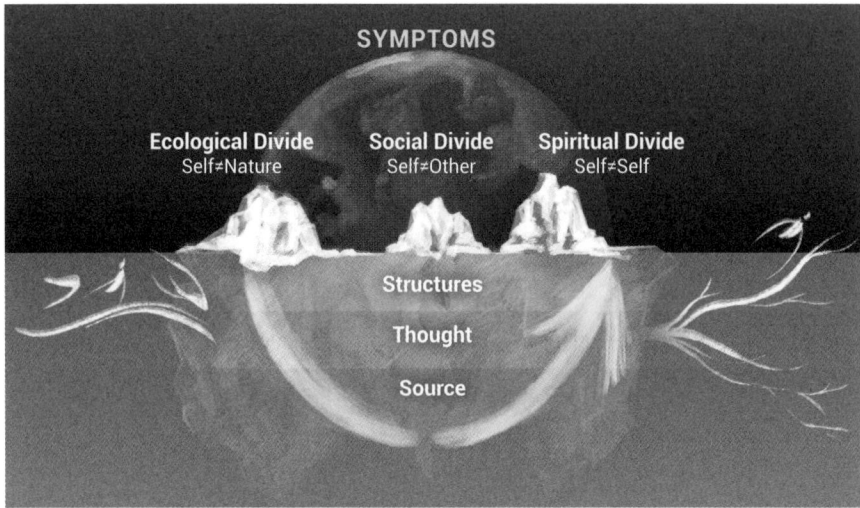

FIGURE 2.1: THE ICEBERG MODEL OF AWARENESS-BASED SYSTEMS CHANGE

amplifying a pandemic of hopelessness by enabling Big Tech to turn human experience into machines of manipulation. This pattern of *organized irresponsibility* needs to be broken.

Second, a system can't be changed unless the consciousness of those who created it and are perpetuating it changes. We cannot address the challenges we are facing with the same thinking that created them:

- We cannot solve our planetary emergency without changing our relationship with the *planet*. We can continue on the current road of destruction, or we can work to change and reshape our systems from extractive to regenerative.
- We cannot end wars and violent conflicts with the same foreign policy logic and mindset that created them. The mindset of *othering* blocks collaboration and movement toward peaceful solutions. We must recognize and accept our interdependency with the world around us.
- We cannot solve the pandemics of loneliness, hopelessness, and depression by applying the same thinking that created them. We will not find

solutions with half-hearted tech fixes that focus on symptoms rather than on the deeper root issues.

Third, we can't change consciousness unless we make a system see and sense itself. As Dayna Cunningham, dean of the Tisch College at Tufts University, has eloquently put it: "When you look into the Wheel of Deep Change, the trick is to 'keep the gaze steady'"[6]—i.e., to not bypass the discomfort of this moment by jumping to denial, blame, or solutionism. When we look into the mirror of the whole system, what do we see? We see the source of all the above problems: *ourselves.* At the same time, though, we can see the possible source of transformative change: *also,* ourselves.

Keeping the gaze steady means relating to the profound sense of loss, sadness, and hopelessness in our current moment. In fact, the hopelessness and pain that many of us, particularly many young people, feel reflects a deeper connection to the pain inflicted on the planet, on others, and perhaps on ourselves. Acknowledging this fact is a profound step forward from the denial of earlier generations.

As we *see ourselves through the eyes of the whole*, we can experience a new *sense of potential* emerging around, among, and through us, a space that in our daily hustle and bustle we tend to miss. In that deeper realm of possibility, the boundaries between me and you, between us and them, begin to shrink:

- By opening our minds, we *shift the source of thought* from silos to systems.
- By opening our hearts, we *shift the source of feeling* from me to we.
- By opening our wills, we *shift the source of agency* from ego to eco.

As our work on systems thinking continues to evolve with the intensifying planetary situation around us, we have been exploring a new metaphor that in many ways may even be a better fit for the current moment and for what in the years ahead is about to come: the metaphor of the social field.

Social Fields: Deep Systems Thinking and Mirroring

A core principle of regenerative agriculture is that the *visible result* (the crop that grows in the soil) is a function of the *quality of the soil* and the *root systems*—in other words, everything that is largely invisible to the eye.

The same principle applies to *social fields*. A social field is defined by both what is above the surface and what is below it. As shown in Figure 2.2, above the surface is the observable, tangible part of the field that we refer to as "social systems." Below the surface of the social soil are the roots and the seeds— that is, the quality of *relationships* and *awareness* that determine how the system works. You could think of a social field as a social system *with interiority* or, perhaps, a social system *with a soul*.

When Otto wrote the book *Theory U*, he used the term Theory U to describe three things: (1) a theory that explains different qualities of human relationships; (2) a method that allows individuals, groups, organizations, and societies to realize their highest potential; and (3) a movement in the making that aims to bridge the three divides (ecological, social, and cultural/spiritual). All social contexts are characterized by a specific *relational quality*. Just as

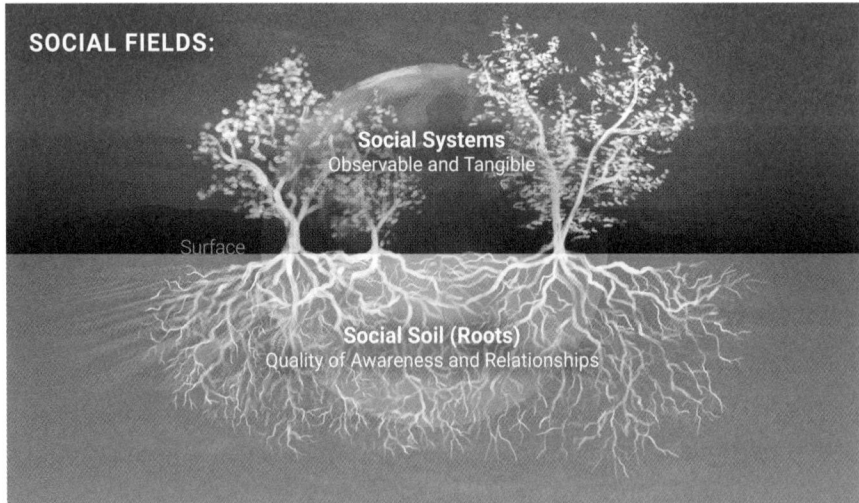

SOCIAL FIELDS:

Social Systems
Observable and Tangible

Surface

Social Soil (Roots)
Quality of Awareness and Relationships

FIGURE 2.2: THE SOCIAL FIELD: SOCIAL SYSTEMS AND SOCIAL SOIL

the quality of the soil determines the quality of the harvest, the underlying quality of the social field—the quality of the relationships in the space—shapes the quality of the practical results in social systems. Relationships include relationships to others, to nature, and to ourselves.

Just as the regenerative farmer focuses on improving the *quality of the soil*, the key task of leaders and changemakers is, in our view, to improve the quality of the *social soil*.

Chapter 3
_____

The Wheel of Deep Change

Looking into the Systems Mirror

W hen applying the Wheel of Deep Change to our current reality, here is what we see: the sectors evolve

- from output- and efficiency-centric (2.0),
- to user- and stakeholder-centric (3.0), and from there
- to eco-system- and regeneration-centric (4.0).

The Upper Hemisphere: Seven Sectors, One Storyline

For example, in agriculture the mainstream focus is on an efficiency or in-dustrialized farming model; next, innovators move toward organic and more sustainable food production, and the current discussion is about regenerative farming. A similar pattern can be found in other sectors. Color Plate 4 tracks the evolution of seven societal sectors through each stage.

Let's take a brief look at each sector. To keep this brief, we will focus on the larger pattern, assuming that many readers can easily fill in the blanks. Also note that mainstream actors in all of these sectors have typically made some movements from 2.0 toward 3.0 modes of operating. Innovators in all these sectors share a similar challenge: what used to make them unique is now what everyone (including the mainstream players in their sectors) claims to be doing, so they need to innovate in ways that are more regenerative and transformative—in short, they need to move from 3.0 to 4.0.

Food and Agriculture

When stepping back and looking at developments of the food and agriculture sector, we see a pattern

- from industrial agriculture: maximizing output and efficiency at great environmental cost,
- to sustainable agriculture: less negative environmental impact,
- to regenerative agriculture: food as the medium for healing planet and people.

All economic and societal development begins (and, in the case of civilizational collapse, ends) with agriculture and the resulting access to food (or the lack thereof, respectively). The mainstream industrial approach to farming still focuses on maximizing output and efficiency at massive environmental cost (estimated at 19 trillion dollars per year globally). But today we see a global movement beginning to take shape around *regenerative* land use and agriculture. This is a hugely important first step. Rethinking and reimagining our agrifood systems is key to addressing the intertwined challenges to water supply, climate, biodiversity, food security, health, and well-being.

Moreover, *regenerative* agriculture has emerged at the heart of a new paradigm, replacing *sustainable* agriculture (and sustainability) as the key concept. The word *regenerative* indicates a higher standard and commitment to the future and encompasses the concept of *social soil* that we introduced in the previous chapter. The work with regenerative farmers in various parts of the world has always been a profound inspiration for everything we do.

Education

Similarly, in education we see a shift

- from "teaching for testing": maximizing test scores at massive developmental cost,
- to student-centered learning: organizing around the questions and journey of the learner,
- to education for human flourishing: whole-person/whole-system learning (head, heart, hand).

Education and learning are central to any transformational path toward sustainable development and a future that is more regenerative, just, and aware. In the face of artificial intelligence (AI) and societal disruptions, it's increasingly obvious that education needs to shift its emphasis from conveying existing knowledge to enabling the next generation to connect to their sources of creativity and potential to co-shape and co-create the future as it emerges.

Moving toward whole-person and whole-system learning involves asking educators to perform a dual shift: The first shift involves the *outer place* of learning; it is a shift from classroom learning toward real-world learning or learning by doing. The second shift involves the *inner place* of learning; it is a shift from the *head* to the *heart* and the *hand*.

In short, innovations in education and learning are beginning to bring the questions and challenges of the world into the classroom, and to create a space where learners are approached not only on an intellectual level but as whole human beings, with emotions and agency. The transformation of learning and education is an emerging movement. We see amazing examples of innovative learning environments in many parts of the world, in particular through our joint work with the Organisation for Economic Co-operation and Development (OECD) on Education for Human Flourishing, which involves various countries that are high performing on several educational outcomes, like Finland, Estonia, and British Columbia in Canada.

Health

The health sector has evolved

- from evidence-based, decontextualized medicine (as the technical foundation),
- to reshaping healthcare delivery systems around the patient journey,
- to strengthening the *sources* of health for human and planetary evolution and well-being (from curative to preventative approaches).

The central question for transforming the healthcare sector is: How do we move from treating the symptoms of illness to strengthening the sources of health and well-being? Many of the leading causes of illness and death in the United States are related to behavior and environmental factors. How do we respond to health challenges without using prescription drugs as the main intervention?[1] Key to a transformation in the healthcare sector will be strengthening the social, ecological, and inner spiritual determinants of well-being that are located in the deeper levels of the social field.

Many of the transformative variables for meeting the key healthcare challenges lie *outside* traditional healthcare—in education, food production, or access to healthy food, for example. Addressing society's systemic health challenges will require organizing and innovating *across* sectoral boundaries. The closer we move to the inner sphere of 4.0 innovation (as shown in Color Plate 4), the more we realize that progress in each sector is intertwined with transformations in the other sectors. For example, adult health and well-being is closely linked to the workplace, which takes us to the next key sector, business.

Business

Business is beginning to shift

- from maximizing a single variable (profitability) at massive social and environmental cost,

- to multistakeholder approaches that optimize environmental, social, and governance metrics,
- to transforming the purpose of business to operating as a force for good.

Business is one of the most powerful forces in today's societies. Many of our societal challenges, but also many of our societal solutions, connect to the economy and the business sector. Let's look at the evolution of the concept of sustainability in business as an example. Early on, many businesses responded to the pressure to integrate sustainability requirements with a focus on resource efficiency—reducing the CO_2 emission by optimizing processes and structure. This shift was often driven by goals of cost reduction and increased profitability. Sustainability also became a topic for public relations or the corporate affairs department, such as under the header of Corporate Social Responsibility (CSR). The next phase of shifting toward sustainability in business concerned the core of the business such as the product innovation process, for example moving from vehicles with combustion engines that run on gasoline to electric vehicles. This phase also included the development of environmental, social, and governance (ESG) reporting practices (3.0). Now some of the most forward-leaning businesses are moving toward the next frontier: transforming the *purpose* of business from shareholder value and profit maximization to operating as a *force for good* (4.0). If successful, this shift will make positive social and environmental impact a critical part of the core business proposition.

Most of today's societal challenges deal in some way with how we frame and structure our economies. If we measure the size of different societal sectors in terms of how much money they operate on, we can see that in the United States in 2023, the size of the non-profit sector was $1.6 trillion, the size of the government sector was around $6 trillion, and the volume of the business sector was a whopping $23 trillion.[2] In other words, for deep transformation and change in twenty-first-century society, the transformation of business is key. It's not enough to criticize economic structures from the outside; all transformative change requires deep immersion, real understanding, and hands-on transformation work from both outside and within the economic sector.

Over the years, we have worked with many companies and their leadership teams. CEOs and business leaders often view their role as overly driven by the drumbeat of quarterly results and short-term expectations from capital markets. This leads to our discussion of the next sector: finance.

Finance

In the finance sector we see a shift

- from extractive and externality blind,
- to ESG and impact investing (partially externality aware),
- to regenerative or transformative finance (fully externality aware).

Let's start with some basics that almost everyone can agree on. There is, broadly speaking, too much money in one place and too little in another. The place where we have too much money is the *extractive economy*. The place where there is too little money is the *regenerative economy*. Finance needs to be reimagined to address the gap between where the vast majority of our capital is deployed and where most people would prefer to see it.

Regenerative or externality-aware finance intentionally seeks investment opportunities and innovative financial products that have a positive impact on society and the planet. Regenerative finance is characterized by transparency and innovative practices that are anchored in an understanding of the social and ecological impact of each financial decision.

In contrast, extractive finance pursues speculative investments that can destabilize the economy by, for example, driving up food prices and hurting those who are already most vulnerable. Financial investments that focus only on maximizing financial returns often come with massive environmental and social costs.

We have been supporting regenerative innovators in finance for many years, through partnering with, among others, the Global Alliance for Banking on Values (GABV).[3] But what is often missing are *connections* between these innovations and different stakeholders, such as policymakers, think tanks, nongovernmental organizations (NGOs), and media.

Another key sector that needs to be part of the process of reshaping our economies is technology, or, in this case, AI. I (Otto) had an interesting experience in Silicon Valley earlier this year. Invited by a large global bank as the final speaker for their high-net-worth clients (i.e., billionaires), I arrived a bit ahead of time and listened to a number of the earlier presentations. What struck me was that all of them shared the same basic storyline: things are great and will be even better in the future; whatever your problem may be, AI and tech are the solution; hence, just trust us with your investments. My gut reaction was: What? Is this a cult? Everyone basically singing the same song?

So, when it was my turn, I could not help but go on a bit of a rant: not everything is great—the planet is going to hell, our societies are falling apart, and our young people are hit by a massive wave of mental health issues—and all three of these things have everything to do with what comes out of Silicon Valley and where you put your money. Just ask yourself how much of your money is funding extractive economic practices and how much you have invested in the regenerative economy. Later in my talk, I invited the audience to a journaling exercise, making them reflect on their deeper intention, the legacy they want to leave behind on this planet, and how that intention is reflected in their current investment portfolio (how much money they have in the extractive and how much in the regenerative economy). What I noticed in the discussion was a range of different responses to these questions. Many, in particular the younger ones, went all in, in full appreciation of this opportunity to step back and look at the systemic impact of investments, while some of the more senior participants shared a more nuanced view on these obviously challenging questions.

Technology and AI

Lastly, in the technology sector, including AI, we see the following shift

- from AI and machine intelligence,
- to machine usefulness,

• to technology that enhances (rather than diminishes) well-being, awareness, and creativity.

Technology has been a key enabler throughout history. Technologies include tools used in the Stone Age (millions of years ago) and tools that enabled the Agricultural Revolution (around 10,000 BCE). The Industrial
Revolution of the eighteenth and nineteenth centuries brought steam power
and electrification. Post–World War II innovations led to industrial petro-
chemicals and automotive mass production. The information technology
(IT) revolution of the late twentieth century produced computers, the internet, and mobile phones. Today, and for the foreseeable future, society will be
shaped by AI in one way or another. At each historical stage, tech started as a
tool and developed into a driver and determinant of societal evolution. Do we
still understand what we are doing? And who is the "we" in that sentence?

The conversation we need to have at this moment should *not* be reduced
to what we usually hear: how AI and *machine intelligence* can replace human
work. Instead, it should focus on, how, as MIT's most recent Nobel Laureate
Simon Johnson has put it, AI can provide *machine usefulness*.[4]

For example, over the past twenty years, large internet platforms (of the
so-called second generation of the internet, or Web 2.0, focusing on user-
generated content) have created astounding wealth in the capital markets
through monopolistic network effects. However, this wealth, along with the
data obtained from internet and social media users, has remained in the
hands of web platforms and data oligarchs, or more accurately, in the hands
of the capital behind them. Says our colleague Lili Xu from China, who has
been a driving force in bringing Theory U and u-lab to China: "the Web 3.0
movement, which peaked around 2021, sought to break the Web 2.0 paradigm through a *build-to-earn* economic model." However, continues Lili,
"most Web 3.0 projects relied too heavily on financial and speculative activities, failing to truly reach the real economy or transform its systems. The
short-lived bubble began to deflate by mid-2022."[5]

In collaboration with a Chinese tech startup in 2020, Lili and colleagues
from a u-lab China team co-created a 4.0 tech infrastructure called MoWa

that is based on a radically distributed ownership and governance model to generate prosperity "for the entire eco-system" rather than a few oligarchs. A multilayered digital ledger, which is a secure, distributed system that tracks transaction data, is used to ensure that "all contributors benefit from shared-intention building and collaborative actions."[6]

What this example demonstrates is how closely the evolution in tech is connected to and shaped by the evolution of governance (see next section). What we urgently need is a conversation about a *new societal contract* around AI and the ownership of data. That social contract should be framed by the question of how to best use the power of AI for the benefit of everyone rather than for a very few plutocrats and empire builders.

The core question is not whether technology and AI are inherently good or evil. It is whether the underlying *intention* of those who create, disseminate, and use these technologies is shaped by ego-system or eco-system awareness and care about the well-being of the whole. The ultimate impact of these technologies is a function of the intentionality of those who create, disseminate, and use them. The quality of the underlying intention determines whether AI-based tech is *diminishing* or *enhancing* well-being, awareness, and creativity in society.

So, why is the evolution in tech and AI still very much stuck in a rut? Because of intention. And that intention manifests through ownership structures. Which brings us to the final leverage point: governance.

Eco-system Governance

Most scholars agree a differentiating factor between humans and other species is the ability to collaborate beyond small-scale tribal boundaries and thus activate collective agency on a scale that no other species can. Over time we have developed this capacity to collaborate, communicate, and act across places and regions. Consequently, the challenge of good governance, how we make decisions collectively, is moving to the forefront of our attention.

The depiction of the recent evolution of governance outlined in this section does not reflect earlier forms of governance. In other words, the actual full journey from those early forms to governance 4.0 has both linear and cyclical aspects. The linear aspects deal with a massive increase of complexity

and of moving beyond planetary boundaries, while the cyclical aspects deal
with some significant parallels between Indigenous and 4.0 forms of governance principles. We would do well to study some of those as inspiration for
changing our current conditions on a larger scale.

The more recent evolution of institutions of governance can be traced as
follows:

- from traditional forms of coordination such as markets and hierarchies
  (2.0),
- to more participatory multistakeholder structures and multilateral institutions (3.0),
- to new forms of collective action from organizing around shared intention and attention (4.0).

All 2.0 forms of governance rely on a set of defined rules. In a democracy
that means every citizen has the right to vote. In an economy people vote with
their money.

But just voting every few years does not create a democracy. And free markets can have massive negative externalities (social and environmental costs
that are not accounted for). The responses to these challenges move us to 3.0
forms of governance systems. Multistakeholder processes, town hall meetings,
participatory budgeting processes, and stakeholder inclusion in evolving regu-
lative frameworks are all examples of 3.0 participatory governance systems.

In his 1927 book *The Public and Its Problems*, John Dewey argues that a democracy is not just a form of governance.[7] A democracy is a collective project
of citizen engagement and co-creation. 3.0 forms of participatory governance
are a first step in that direction.

When we begin to think about the necessary innovations the current
polycrisis calls for, we see that many of these have already been prototyped
by forward-looking organizations. The financial institutions that are part of
the Global Alliance for Banking on Values are one example, as are many of the
businesses certified as B corps (benefit corporations).[8] These institutions are
rethinking their *purpose*, grounding it in a shared intention. Quipu, a digital,

decentralized fintech company in Colombia, was founded to offer financial solutions for small businesses in the informal economy, which are often unable to get loans from traditional banks. The founders of Quipu wanted to create a positive societal impact by helping the informal economy. Similarly, BRAC Bank in Bangladesh, which also was founded to reach those excluded from or neglected by traditional banking options, created financial products that serve illiterate entrepreneurs.

What all these examples have in common is a 4.0 shift in governance where the actions of all key actors are anchored in a shared intention to further the well-being of the society as a whole.

Over the past several years, our Presencing Institute colleagues have been working with thirty UN Country Teams and Humanitarian Country Teams who respond to urgent crises around the world and have designed leadership labs to help these teams to meet the UN's Sustainable Development Goals (SDGs). Becky Buell, our colleague who helped launch these labs, reflects:

> Most people feel that their systems—whether organizations, sectors or societies—are too big, too complex, or too entrenched to change. But what we saw over and over again in our work with the UN was that when people connect deeply to their individual and collective purpose—that core intention of alleviating suffering and building prosperous societies for all that led them to want to work with the UN in the first place—then things start to shift. They stopped waiting for the promised "UN Reform" to take place and *they became the reform themselves*, taking actions large and small that begin to bring that aspired future into being.

As one UN senior leader said, "The Lab confirmed something important: you must start building the new system whilst the old one is still there. The new system will destroy the old one eventually when the time is right. An old door will close only if you dare open a new one . . . before the old one is closed!"[9] These leadership labs build understanding and skills in the practical applications of systems thinking, innovation, and transformative leadership. New types of crises call for new types of solutions, a belief shared by one of the UN participants, who said: "In our institutional context we are trying to solve 4.0 challenges with 2.0 methods and tools." Another added: "We are being encouraged to shoot for the moon while some of us are still driving a donkey cart."[10]

The evolution from 2.0 to 4.0 forms of governance is a journey of interiorization. It's a journey from *exterior* mechanisms of coordination to the acquisition of complementary *interior* mechanisms organized around *shared attention* and *intention*. Together they can catalyze collective action.

There are numerous local examples. We see them in our neighborhoods and in our cities. We also see them occasionally in larger contexts. Think about the 2015 Paris Climate Agreement, an example of national governments coming together and coming to an agreement. Or think about the 30-by-30 initiative, a movement for governments to designate 30 percent of the Earth's land and ocean area as protected areas by 2030. Launched by the High Ambition Coalition for Nature and People in 2020, more than 190 countries had signed on by August 2024.

From Ego to Eco—from Polycrisis to Polysystemic Regeneration

When farmers and citizens collaborate on regenerative and localized food systems; when patients, citizens, and healthcare providers collaborate on strengthening the sources of good health and well-being; when educators reimagine and reshape their relationships with learners and schools to better help them to co-sense and co-activate their creative capacities; when entrepreneurs rethink the purpose of business as a way to better benefit society; when investors and financial institutions rethink the purpose of money as a force for good; and when politicians and public officeholders ground their actions and initiatives in the long-term flourishing of their communities, they are creating ripple effects within their respective sectors. If all of these changes were to happen simultaneously they would create a *groundswell* of transformation that affects all sectors, all systems, and all geographies. This would signal a profound shift from a silo to a systems view, or, as we like to say, from an *ego-system* to an *eco-system* awareness.

We're not using the term *eco-system* to refer to just the natural world or just a social network of stakeholders. *Eco-system awareness* describes a deepened understanding that the survival and well-being of all beings and the living planet are inseparable from each other.

Color Plate 4 depicts the shift from ego-system to eco-system awareness as an evolution from the outer spheres (1.0 and 2.0) to the middle and inner spheres of deep change (3.0 and 4.0). The figure may look a bit complex, but the underlying logic and structure is very simple and clear: *The evolution of our institutions and societal systems can be seen as the manifestation of an **evolving human consciousness** that moves from ego to eco.* In other words, our modern social systems have been evolving from an input–output logic (operating systems [OS] 1.0 and 2.0: ego) to one that revolves around user and stakeholder concerns (3.0) and from there to one that expands human awareness and intentionality to the well-being of the entire eco-system (4.0: eco).[11]

We see this evolution from an ego- to an eco-consciousness underway in all sectors, with variations in speed and shape. And as always in developmental models, moving from 2.0 to 3.0 and from there to 4.0 does not mean abandoning the earlier stages. The core functionalities of the earlier stages continue to exist in the later ones, but they are embedded in a new context, just as the core functionalities of an older operating system do not cease to exist when you upgrade your device.

An outdated OS on one of our devices, like a smart phone, can interfere with newer applications that we want to use. Likewise, the new challenges that we face across our societal sectors require us to upgrade our existing operating systems. But upgrading *societal operating systems* is of course much more complex and requires us to shift our attention to the qualities of our awareness and relationships, represented by the lower half of the Wheel of Deep Change (Color Plate 4).

When leaders, activists, innovators, and their initiatives embark on a 4.0 journey toward regenerative and eco-systemic ways of operating, something interesting begins to happen: *the boundaries between the sectors* open up and offer *a space for co-creative convergence and emergence.* The interior sphere of the Wheel becomes a new space for connection, regeneration, and profound personal and polysystemic renewal. When educators begin to reconnect with *nature as a teacher* for human flourishing, when farmers adopt regenerative cultivation practices, when health system experts rediscover regenerative food processes as a medium for healing the Earth, when businesses begin to build innovations that serve the whole, these sectors are no longer separate. They live, breathe, and thrive together. Boundaries between the sectors begin to dissolve. *What we see on these occasions is the emergence of a new sphere of profound regeneration and renewal.*

Foldout Color Plate 1 depicts the overview of the entire discussion in this chapter and book: two hemispheres (upper half: social systems, and lower half: social soil) and four circular spheres of evolutionary gravitation from 1.0 in the outer sphere to 4.0 in the inner sphere. When people and their initiatives venture into that inner sphere of *convergence*, they begin to address their challenges and issues by

- moving from extractive to regenerative practices;
- moving from ego-system to eco-system awareness;
- moving from human and planetary degradation to human and planetary flourishing; and
- moving from reenacting the past to co-sensing and co-creating the emerging future.

But because this evolutionary pull toward 4.0 is mostly hidden and remains the most important, least-well-told story of our time, it currently lacks any of the necessary support structures that is needed to actualize its massive dormant potential.

Building and cultivating support structures in this 4.0 space is a precondition for success on our journey from extraction to regeneration, from degradation to flourishing, and from ego to eco.

But why doesn't the evolution from 1.0 and 2.0 to 4.0 happen faster? What is holding us back? We believe it's because we are looking at it the wrong way. We haven't shifted our attention from tangible social systems (upper half of the Wheel) to the intangible side of the social field: the *social soil*—the quality of our awareness and relationships. We're not paying attention to the entire lower half of the Wheel.

The Lower Half of the Wheel: Practices for Cultivating the Social Soil

The lower half of the Wheel of Deep Change contains seven practices that are the foundation of transformative leadership and change. In much of our public discourse, and in organizational and institutional work, the primary focus tends to be on visible outcomes, while the less visible qualities of the social field are ignored. We don't make the connection between the two halves: the quality of the tangible things that we *see* is a function of the quality of the intangible conditions that we don't see: the social soil that nourishes what grows from it.

If social fields are social systems with a soul, then the soul is what's lost when we disregard the soil. The soil of the social field contains our relationships and our awareness, both individual and collective.

In that interior space we see the different qualities of the *social soil*, the different qualities of *awareness* or *consciousness*. But what does this really mean? What changes do we see with our *eyes* when the awareness in a group shifts from one state to another or from one quality to another? How does a shift like this manifest? How do we know that we know?

A shift in awareness in any social field manifests as a shift in *relationships*. An improvement in the quality of a relationship can be attributed to greater trust or more effective collaboration. Simply put, the shift can be measured by the degree of separation—by the degree to which boundaries in a social field erode and eventually collapse.

And that shift can be experienced. Our South African colleague Marian Goodman described the experience like this:

> You see a different human being. There is a different relationship there. . . .
> It has something to do with the social skins that we wear. We mostly wear
> quite thick skins—the layers that protect us or "hide" us, and I don't mean
> that in a bad way. . . . When the quality of the social space is held well,

without judgment and in safety and confidentiality, we get a chance to connect with the being behind the social skin. Once [you are] connected to that, you cannot go back. Even if you go back to a normal, lighter human interaction, it stays with you.[12]

Reintegrating the Wheel:
Bending the Beam of Attention Back

Changemakers and leaders in all institutions deal with so-called network leadership challenges. They need to align partners and stakeholders who often are part of other organizations, or communities, with possibly conflicting goals—in other words, they need to influence and align people who do not report to them.

How can changemakers and leaders bring about change without formal authority? The only way to effect change in such a situation is to shift the *quality* of *relationships*. You do that by shifting the quality of *listening* and *communication*. In other words, the types of challenges that leaders and changemakers face "above the soil" require us to slow down and bend the beam of observation back onto our own qualities of listening and conversation, back onto the lower half of the Wheel (Foldout Color Plate 1).

The ability to bend the beam of attention back onto ourselves is what makes it possible to activate deeper levels of leadership and human development.

The interdependence between the two halves of the Wheel of Deep Change applies across systems, sectors, and geographies. We experience the connection between the two hemispheres of the Wheel as citizens and in our relationships with friends, educators, family, and others. We experience it in how we relate to each other, but also in how we relate to our planet and to ourselves. In all these dimensions we know that bending the beam of attention is the key to slowing down and accessing our deeper sources of knowing. Once we do that, a new set of possibilities begins to open up.

The bending of the beam of attention is the *one and only portal* into the deep structure of systems change. Democratizing access to the conditions that will enable this kind of shift is a crucial task for our societies.

Core Practices

As we transition from the visible to the less visible parts of our social fields and systems, the nature of what matters shifts. Above the soil, the visible systems, concepts, frameworks, and measurable results are the main currency. But when it comes to implementing those concepts to bring about deep change, the main currency shifts to *practices*. Practices are what we do every day. Practices are what we embody when we show up, the way we are present in the situation at hand. Through cultivation of our practices, we increase our capacity to activate our agency, both individually and collectively.

The seeds of these practices and capacities are inside each of us. Some of them are already well developed, while others might need more attention. These practices can be learned, cultivated, and shared. For example, at the Presencing Institute we set up reflection groups for practitioners in different contexts and locations to allow them to share their personal experiences with these practices and to learn from each other.

To that end, this book introduces and describes **seven core practices of cultivating the social soil**, shifting how we relate to each other from ego to eco, from extraction to regeneration, from toxicity to healing.

Many of the practices will be familiar and they work as an ensemble. They include the following:

becoming aware: bending the beam of attention back onto ourselves

listening: holding the space within; listening with our *minds* and *hearts* wide *open*

dialogue: holding spaces for making systems see and sense themselves

presencing: holding the space to meet the future that stays in need of us in the now

co-imagination: holding spaces for crystallizing the future that we want to create

co-creation: holding spaces for exploring the future by doing

eco-system governance: holding spaces for coordinating around shared intentions

These seven practices are fully introduced and described in detail in chapter 5. They allow us to move from the more traditional operating systems (the outer spheres) to more complex ways of operating (inner spheres) that our current situation and planetary polycrisis call for (see Foldout Color Plate 1).

Two Forces, Two Attractors

This journey from 2.0 to 4.0, from siloed to more systemic ways of operating, is one trajectory and attractor or evolutionary center of gravity that we are experiencing now. It's a journey from ego to eco in the evolution of our societal structures, in the evolution of human consciousness in response to increasing complexity and interdependence. Individuals, organizations, and communities are beginning to operate from a broader awareness, one that moves beyond the small ego and includes the well-being of the larger ecosystem that all of us are a part of.

But there is another story and evolutionary attractor as well. In fact, many people are experiencing the current moment as *diverging* forces pulling us in two different directions, adding to the current sense of ambiguity and confusion. One is pulling us toward the inner sphere of convergence (4.0). The other one is pulling us toward the outer sphere of amplified control that in Figure 3.1 is depicted as 1.0.

Figure 3.1 depicts the various symptoms and issues that mark the core aspects of our current polycrisis.

These symptoms are well known. We'll do a quick flyover, beginning with Technology (at 2 p.m.) and moving counterclockwise around the Wheel.

Technology

Three unintended side effects from our first encounter with technology (in the form of social media) include *mass misinformation*, *mass polarization*, and *mass depression*, as discussed previously. They emerge when profit is prioritized over the well-being of societies and people. Why is social media a trillion-dollar industry? Because it works, at least in the short term. Much of Big Tech—or to be more precise, Big Social Media—runs on a business model that makes

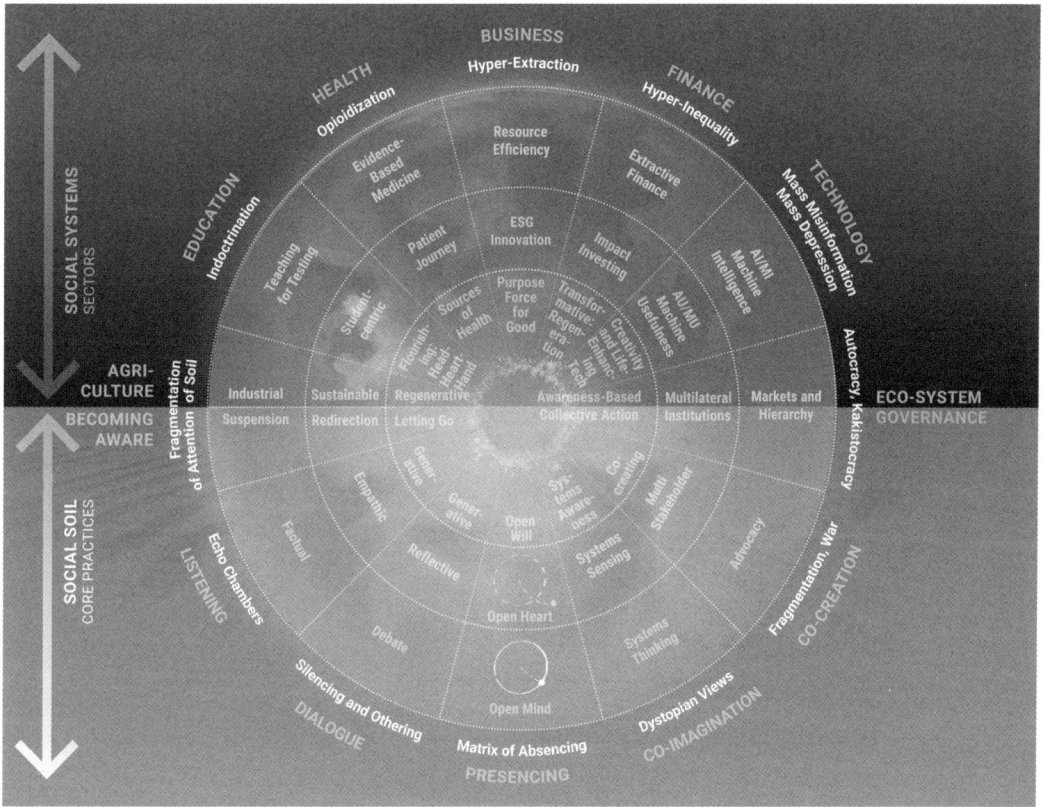

FIGURE 3.1: MATRIX OF ABSENCING

money by converting human experience via data analytics into outputs designed to effectively manipulate human behavior on the level of the collective.

The underlying operating system runs on what Shoshana Zuboff calls "epistemological inequality."[13] Picture two rooms that are separated by a one-way mirror. In one room there are thirty to forty people with full access to all the data in the individual profiles of billions of people; they are profiles of vulnerabilities that allow that small group to influence or manipulate the behavior of the billions. In the other room are, say, 3.6 billion people (the current user base of platforms owned by Meta, to use one example)—basically the rest of us—who can't see their own data, let alone everyone else's, or the underlying algorithms. The one-way mirror gives those thirty to forty people unrestricted access to the rest of us. That's the face of epistemological inequality. A very small group of people *controls* the behavior of the many by restricting their access to their own data, which, if visible, would allow them to *retake control* of their own agency.

The business model of social media is based on injecting junk into the system—misinformation, designed to activate anger, hate, or fear—via our social media feeds into our awareness, to extract the one thing that tech companies really want: our attention. It leaves behind a severely damaged human and social eco-system.

Finance

Hyper-inequality is amplified through a similar shadow side in our financial economy "Junk," such as toxic financial instruments, is injected into the economic process to extract what most financial institutions' wealth holders want: high financial returns. In many cases it leaves behind a severely damaged social, economic, and ecological eco-system.

To back up this claim, here is an interesting data point. Between 1975 and 2018, the wealth transfer from the bottom 90 percent to the top 1 percent of people in the United States was dramatic. According to the authors of a 2020 RAND study, it was a transfer of $47 trillion.[14] The study explored what would have happened if the more equitable income distributions of the three decades following World War II (1945 through 1974) had continued in the decades after 1974. They found that the bottom 90 percent of people in the United States would have received $47 trillion more. Instead, almost the entire amount went straight to the top 1 percent.

Business

Hyper-extraction is another polycrisis-related trend and phenomenon. A good illustration is fracking by the fossil fuel industry. Fracking is the injection of junk (chemicals) under extreme pressure into the body of our planet to extract oil and gas. The process severely damages Earth's eco-systems.

Health

Opioidization is one manifestation of how the polycrisis shows up in our health sectors. Opioidization applies the same process and logic of fracking to our health system: junk (addictive painkillers like OxyContin) is injected under extreme pressure (through aggressive marketing and sales strategies) into the health system to generate high profits. This leaves behind a severely damaged human and social eco-system and contributes to addiction and death from opioid-involved overdoses. There are hundreds of thousands of victims in the United States alone.

Education

Teaching for testing, such as making students memorize correct answers for multiple choice tests, is injected under high pressure into the minds of our students to extract the one thing that educators (and parents) want: high test scores. The results are young people with shockingly high rates of mental health issues, including anxiety disorders and depression.

Looking at the upper hemisphere of symptomatic expressions of our current polycrisis, we can see a pattern of extraction and degradation in *all of the sectors.*

Turning our attention now to the lower hemisphere of the Wheel—that is, to the quality of the social soil—we see another set of symptoms:

Degradation of soil and fragmentation of attention: What the degradation of soil does to the health of the planet, the fragmentation of attention does to human well-being. Both processes undermine the basic capacity for flourishing through extractive practices.

Echo chambers: We know that social media algorithms and feeds filter information, sending us into echo chambers that block our access to views that are different from our own.

Othering and silencing: These lead to "cancel culture" on both the left and the right. We remove viewpoints we profoundly disagree with rather than engaging with them.

Dystopian views: Dystopian views of the future are omnipresent. We know what we *don't* want our future to look like. But the conversation about the future we *do* want is crowded out.

Fragmentation and war: In many respects, we are living in a society that is falling apart, into pieces that have lost the capacity to listen, converse, and co-create together. Instead, we see increasing violence against those we disagree with and those who are most marginalized in society.

Autocracy and kakistocracy: The rise of autocracy, the rule of one, and kakistocracy, rule by the worst or the *least qualified*, are other features of the polycrisis that we see when we look into the collective mirror of the Wheel (Figure 3.1 and Foldout Color Plate 1).

The Matrix of Absencing

Are these symptoms of the polycrisis really different problems and issues, or are they expressions of one and the same problem? Leaning into the latter view, we have long searched for an appropriate term to describe the collective symptoms. The three prominent characteristics of the polycrisis are (1) extractive modes of operating, (2) social and mental architectures of fragmentation and disintegration, and (3) unilateral control and reactive loops—that is, loss of presencing-based agency. What's the bottom line? Is it a matrix of manipulation, of mechanization (turning us into machines), of absencing, or of all the above? Whatever we call it, it represents a state of awareness that is severely diminishing people's capacity to access their deepest sources of presence, agency, and freedom.

Antidotes: Our Dormant Superpowers

As you have probably noticed, the seven leadership practices can be seen as direct antidotes to the challenges the polycrisis poses.

The *practice of becoming aware*, of bending the beam of attention back onto ourselves, is the ultimate antidote against the onslaught on our attention that is happening around and between us.

The *practice of listening*, of holding the space within and listening with our minds and hearts wide open, is the ultimate antidote to getting stuck inside our own echo chambers. As filter bubbles continue to be created online and political polarization increases, the practice of generative listening is a key tool for staying connected—with other people, with a situation as it unfolds, and with yourself.

The *practice of dialogue* is about holding open the space for thinking together, in order to allow systems to see themselves. The more the viewpoints among participants differ, the more cultural assumptions diverge, the more relevant the conversational format of dialogue tends to be.

The *practice of presencing* is that of stopping, of connecting with our sources of stillness and inner knowing, which allows the *future that stays in need of us* to enter our awareness. With that subtle shift, our sense of who we really are is heightened and strengthened. Under our current condition of absencing, this practice is critical.

The *practice of co-imagination* is about dreaming forward together, about holding a space to generate images of the future that we want to create. The more our mental, cultural, and spiritual spaces are filled with dystopian views of the future, the more important this practice and capacity will turn out to be.

The *practice of co-creation* is about holding the space to explore the future by doing, or prototyping and iterating based on feedback. In an age of conflict and blame, the capacity to create together, across boundaries, is an essential tool.

The *practice of eco-system governance* is about advancing our existing coordination mechanisms by organizing around shared attention and intention to catalyze collective agency. In a world regressing from multilateralism to bilateralism and unilateral control, advancing our governing intelligence is essential to increasing the intelligence of our governance systems.

The seeds of these seven capacities are already inside of us; every human being has them, though they tend to be largely dormant. With the help of these seven practices these seeds can grow and, after more cultivation, turn into our superpowers for navigating this century's challenges of change. Many of these challenges, and the disruptions that are driving them, are already out of our control. What, then, is *in* our control? In three words, it is *how we respond*. Everything else is secondary.

Evolution as the Manifestation of an Evolving Human Consciousness

This chapter tells two stories that are conflicting and to some degree clashing. One is the story of the destruction caused by the polycrisis. The other describes the evolutionary journey toward the inner sphere of regeneration and convergence. Both of these stories are intimately intertwined. Moving from one to the other requires a journey that begins with the awareness that we are moving into the wrong direction, a feeling that roughly 69 percent of humankind shares.[15]

This feeling invites us on a quest to take back control by deepening our *attention* (from shallow to generative listening), by deepening our *relationships* (from polarization to partnering), and by deepening our *agency* (activating our dormant superpowers).

Foldout Color Plate 1 summarizes the argument of this chapter: that the patterns of *societal evolution are manifestations of an evolving human consciousness* that is moving from ego to eco, from 1.0 and 2.0 structures (focused on control and efficiency) to 3.0 or 4.0 structural forms (focused on stakeholder and eco-system agency).

The journey from polycrisis to polysystemic regeneration and transformation is a journey from the outer to the inner spheres of the social field. To advance on this journey we need to learn how to shift the *source* of our thinking from the head to the heart (from systems thinking to systems sensing and presencing) and how to deepen the learning cycle from reflecting the past to sensing and actualizing the emerging future.

But that is only one of the two scenarios and pathways that are available to us at this juncture. The other one concerns the scenario of absencing that we described earlier. It's a story of dealing with the same set of challenges but responding to them with a different operating model. What is the ultimate difference between these two operating models, which are depicted in Foldout Color Plate 1 as the outermost and the innermost spheres? The ultimate difference is whether or not our response is rooted in the cultivation of the social soil (by deploying some version of the seven leadership practices). Accordingly, our future will either involve exteriorized control and diminished human agency (absencing) or interiorized control and enhanced full actualization of our agency. Those are two possible pathways that we face at this evolutionary juncture. Which one are we going to choose?

Chapter 4

Presencing, Absencing, and Fourth-Person Knowing

There is nothing that arises in our experience that we are not big enough to hold.
—MARIAN GOODMAN

A t this point, you might be thinking, *OK, the challenges are big. And so are the opportunities for profound regeneration.* But how does all of this actually work? How are we all going to learn to operate *from the future* that Martin Buber told us "stays in need of us"?[1]

As humans we can relate to the future in two primary ways: one is through the knowing of the head. Here we have tools such as trend analysis, expert forecasting, and other methods of anticipating what is ahead. The second way (and these two ways can go hand in hand) is through the *knowing of the heart*. We lean into the current reality and sense a potential, an opportunity or something that lies ahead of us. In our research we heard many entrepreneurs, innovators, and thought leaders describing this one way or another. Presencing is a method for combining these two paths and especially for giving the second path a process that allows us to step into the new that we cannot yet capture with the mind. This second path is not just about circumstances and trends, though those things can be part of it and through us. It establishes a *direct connection* to the future potential that is emerging in the now. This connection can be created individually, but also collectively—through groups and organizations and even on a societal level.

But what is needed to connect to this path is a cultivation of our deeper sensing capacities, by using our heart as an *organ of perception*. We describe this process as learning and leading *from* a future that is emerging.

Acting and Sourcing from the Emerging Future

In our work on presencing we deploy the word *future* differently than most people do. When people talk about the future, they are usually referring to what will happen at a much later time and place, something that is far away and often separate from them. When *we* use the word *future*, we mean something far more personal and immediate: we're talking about what is happening right here, right now, through each of us. Presencing focuses on the future that is about to unfold from this very moment. And right in this moment, we have the option to connect to emergent possibilities or to ignore them. We have learned from entrepreneurs, innovators, and changemakers that the making of the future is personal. The future is a possibility that is *looking at us* because it *depends* on us to manifest. Whether consciously or subconsciously, every moment we are choosing whether to limit the focus of our attention to what's already fully in the realm of visibility—aboveground—or whether to broaden and deepen our attention to what is emerging from the less visible layers underground.

We are not talking about something that rarely happens and only for a select few. We are talking about a widely distributed phenomenon that is experienced by many but is rarely talked about because (a) we lack the right language and framing, and (b) it may come across as a bit weird.

In our work with changemakers and initiatives in many parts of the world, we have experienced a deeply personal sense of a future potential that is

Color Plates

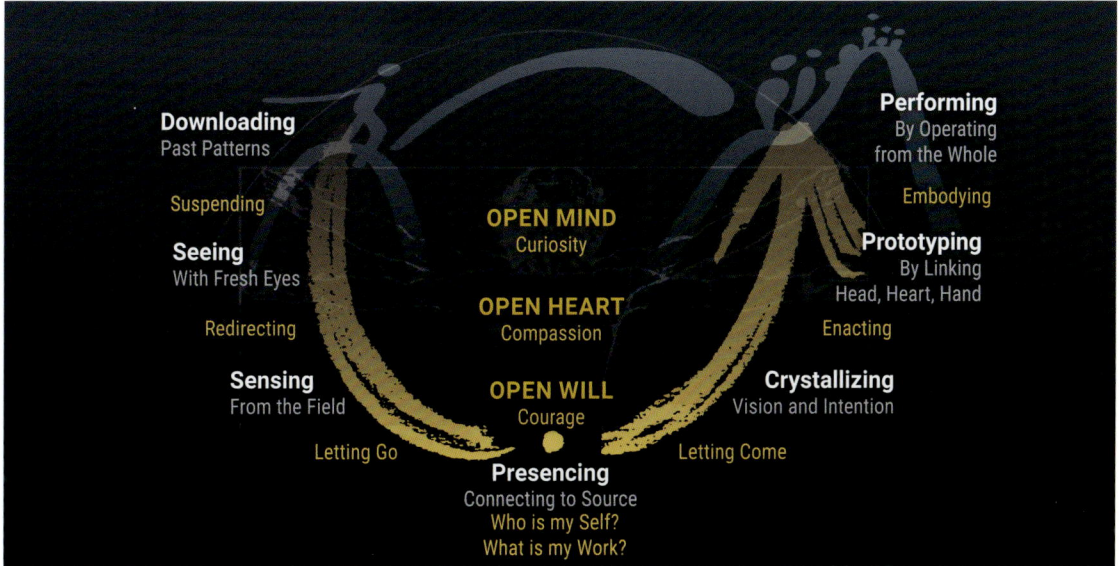

COLOR PLATE 1: THEORY U I (ORIGINAL VERSION)

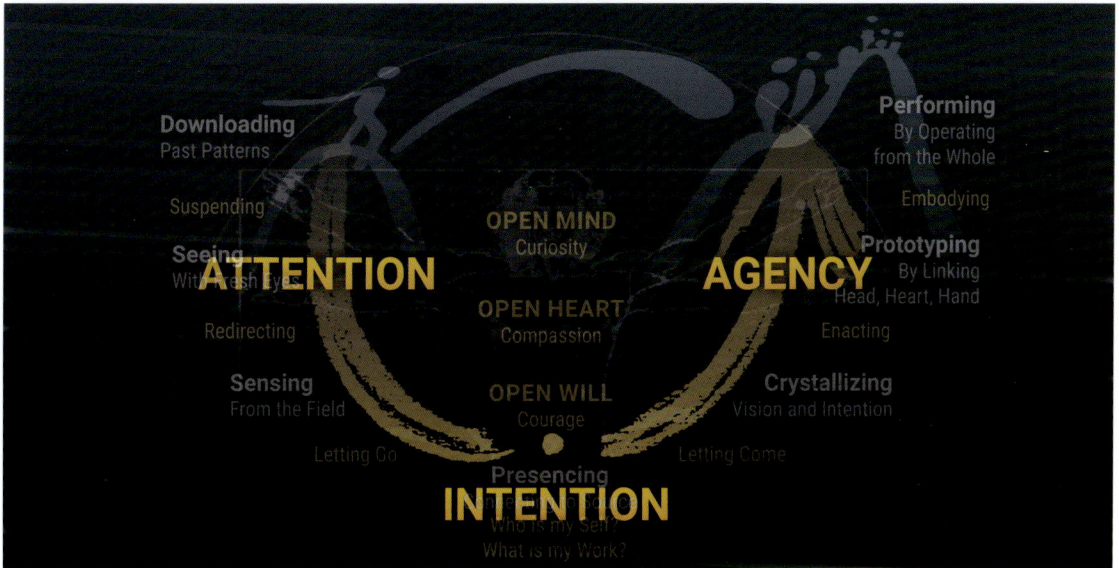

COLOR PLATE 2: THEORY U II (ALIGNING ATTENTION, INTENTION, & AGENCY)

FOLDOUT COLOR PLATE 1: THE WHEEL OF DEEP CHANGE (*UPPER HALF*: SOCIAL SYSTEMS, *LOWER HALF*: SOCIAL SOIL) AS A MANIFESTATION OF AN EVOLVING CONSCIOUSNESS FROM EGO TO ECO (FOUR SPHERES)

FOLDOUT COLOR PLATE 2: PRESENCING INSTITUTE: U-SCHOOL, U-IMPACT, U-RESEARCH (ARTWORK BY KELVY BIRD AND OLAF BALDINI)

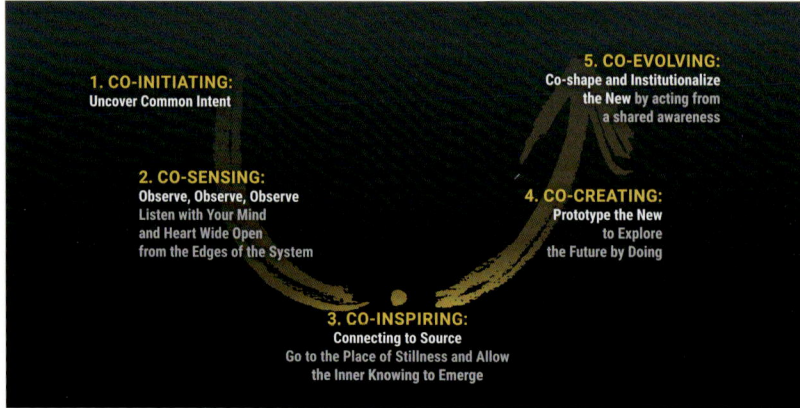

COLOR PLATE 3: THE U IN PRACTICE: FIVE MOVEMENTS, ONE PROCESS

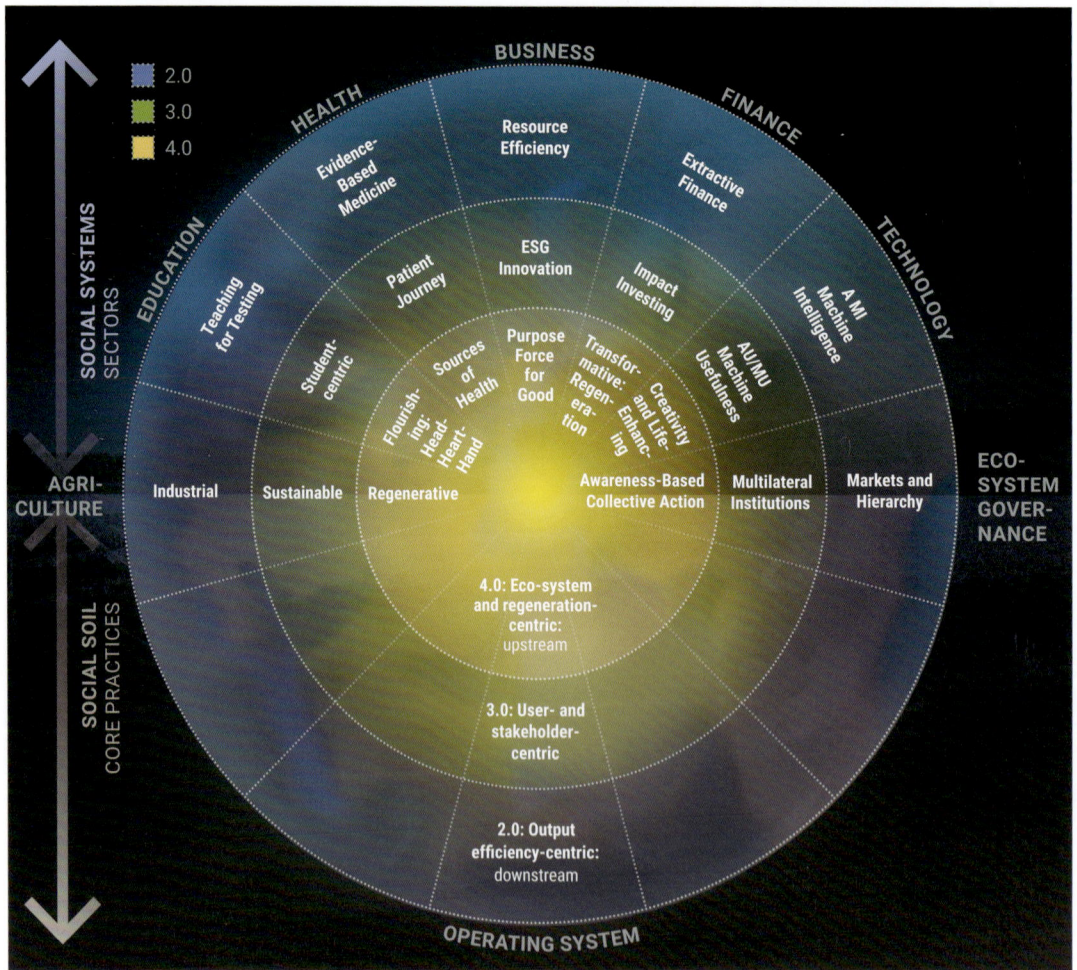

COLOR PLATE 4: THE EVOLUTION OF SOCIETAL SECTORS (*UPPER HALF*) AS A FUNCTION OF UPDATING THE OPERATING SYSTEM (*LOWER HALF*)

PRESENCING I

u-research
Generating Kno
and Tools
Cross-Discipli
Science, Social Arts, Sys

u-school:
Building Capacity for
Transforming Systems and Self
Cross-Intelligences:
Mind, Heart, Will

Leading from
Emerging Fu
Shifting Consciou
From Ego to E

BECOMING AWARE

Seven Leadership
For Cultivating the S

LISTENING

CO-SENSING DIALOGUE

PRESENCIN

NSTITUTE

n:
wledge

e:
ems Change

u-impact:
Empowering Organizational
and Eco-system Transformation
Cross-Sectors:
Business, Government, Civil Society

the
:ure

sness:
:o

ECO-SYSTEM GOVERNANCE

Practices
ocial Soil

CO-CREATING

CO-IMAGINING

G

connected to their, and our, forward journey, to what we are here to do. Once established, this sense does not go away. It guides us. It's a connection between me and my higher future potential, my higher Self, between my current self and that aspect of my Self that is connected to that future potential. Paying attention to that *connection* enables us to tune into our calling. It helps us to sense resonances that are critical for navigating our path forward into uncharted territory that is now ahead of us.

"Because I Can't Not Do It"

When reflecting with creators, entrepreneurs, and innovators on the triumphs and unavoidable setbacks that are part of most creative journeys—the "road of trials"—we asked them, "What kept you going?" The response we often heard was: "Because I can't not do it!"[2]

Because I can't not do it is not part of a mental framework. It's not exactly a feeling. It's a state of our will, a state of being *locked in* to our intention. And that is a force that can make mountains move, as it quite frequently does.

What barrier keeps us from fully activating our own intention and agency? What keeps us from more fully locking in to what we believe in and want to make happen?

What's missing is not the individual intention itself. What's missing, we believe, are the right *spaces* that allow us to sense, surface, clarify, and activate our intentions, both individually and collectively.

The need for these spaces, where we can find our agency, is the most important lesson from the u-lab, the online/offline activation platform that we run. The most common feedback from participants is that it was the lab's personal *and* global holding spaces that helped them to clarify their deeper intentions and take the first steps toward realizing them. These first steps are usually baby steps, "micro" actions that help shift one's inner orientation from merely contemplating the future to realizing it. Our colleague Eva Pomeroy, research lead at the Presencing Institute, describes this as activating "action confidence."[3] Action confidence is not the same as performance confidence, or the ability to do something well. Action confidence is the capacity to step into something new. And this first step is often the hardest. But once it is done, the next steps follow. We sometimes compare this to hiking a mountain. It feels like a huge task at the beginning, but then each step makes the next one easier.

Beginnings Matter

The first step toward activating our agency is critical and often takes longer than anticipated, mostly because we're still figuring things out. But beginnings matter. Like one seed on the ground, it's very small, seemingly insignificant, and almost invisible to the eye—yet its entire future potential is present in that kernel.

New initiatives and projects are like plants and trees in the sense that there is a visible part above the ground—the objectives, team members, processes, etc.—and there is an invisible part below the ground that concerns the quality of attention, intention, and relationships: the social soil.

But before we dive more deeply into these conditions through a few stories, let's refine the underlying question. The essential observation in this book is that the visible part of our current reality depends on the invisible ground: the social soil. The quality of the invisible social soil determines the quality of the outcomes of our actions. *How can we make the invisible side of transformation and change—the lower hemisphere of the Wheel of Deep Change—more visible and accessible to everyone?* We might also ask: *How can it be made more accessible to our inquiry and understanding?*

When we co-founded the Presencing Institute, our intention was not to build another big-project machine, even though some large-scale projects are a necessary part of the work we do. The reason we founded it is to co-invent new methods, tools, and enabling spaces for deep systems change and then to make them available to an emerging planetary movement that cuts across all sectors.

The Blind Spot

In the research that led to the development of Theory U, Otto interviewed the biologist and cognitive neuroscientist Francisco Varela, first in 1996 and then again in 2000.

> When I met him at his research lab in Paris, Varela claimed that there is a "methodological blind spot" in Western science. "The problem is not that we don't know enough about the brain," he said. "The problem is that we don't know how we access experience."[4]
>
> In 2000, roughly a year before he passed away, I went back to Paris to learn more about what he had found out about illuminating this blind spot. In that second interview he told me that he had identified three methods: psychological introspection, phenomenology, and meditation. He had synthesized the essence of these methods into "a core process of becoming aware."[5] That core process consists of three gestures or turns:
>
> - **Suspension:** the ability to suspend habits of judgment and see with fresh eyes
> - **Redirection:** the ability to redirect your attention from the object to the source
> - **Letting go:** the ability to let go of the old, to be fully present, and to allow something new to emerge
>
> When I left Varela's office, I knew I had been handed a gift. I knew that I had seen the process that he described many times: from the suspension of judgment (starting to listen), to redirecting our attention (seeing a situation through another person's eyes), to letting go (opening up to what is emerging). In my case, though, I had seen it in workshops and team development processes, while Varela had explored it by observing individuals using meditative and phenomenological practices.

Today, we would describe that gift like this: experience is not what happens to us—*experience is what we do with what happens to us*. And that inner doing is specified by the three gestures of *suspension, redirection,* and *letting go*.

As helpers, leaders, changemakers, educators, entrepreneurs, therapists, journalists, activists, and civil servants, we are repeatedly thrown into new and disruptive situations that require us to dissolve our old, frozen frameworks and respond in new ways that align with emerging future possibilities because disruption means something is ending, and something else is beginning. But *how* do we do that exactly?

What we have learned over the years is that there are three important gateways for co-sensing and operating from the emerging future. These can be read as a rearticulation of the three turns that Varela described. It's a rearticulation that is framed from the viewpoint of the practitioner:

- Access your not-knowing.
- Access your discomfort.
- Access your non-action.

As visualized in Figure 4.1, these three attentional areas are underrated in our current leadership and learning culture, while their three counterparts, knowledge, comfort, and action, tend to be overrated.

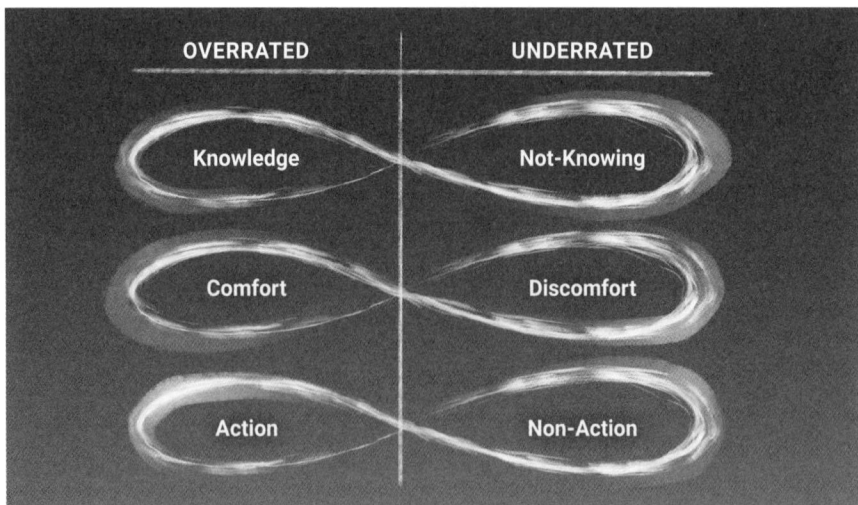

FIGURE 4.1: THREE THINGS OVERRATED; THREE THINGS UNDERRATED

Access Your Not-Knowing

One of the most useful pieces of advice we ever got from Otto's mentor at MIT, Ed Schein, was to "access your ignorance." It is so useful in part because it is so counterintuitive. Usually—say, in a conversation—you gravitate to topics that you are familiar with, that you know a lot about. But Ed says no, do the opposite. He suggests that in any situation of helping, if you gravitate with your attention and inquiry toward your not-knowing, all your questions and interventions will be a lot more effective. It always works. It's true that sometimes it is useful and appropriate to add your knowledge to a conversation. But it's also true that most of the things that really matter—like the future—we don't really know. The deeper we move into our current age of disruption, the more important the principle of "accessing your not-knowing" or "accessing your ignorance" will be because it allows us to open up to the flow of future possibilities.[6] The emphasis in Theory U on sensing and several of the seven leadership practices introduced in the next chapter focus squarely on accessing our not-knowing.

Access Your Discomfort

Accessing your not-knowing is not always comfortable. But staying inside your comfort zone can be hugely problematic and limiting to your course of action as a changemaker, as a leader, or as a friend or mentor. Any professional in change management and leadership knows that as long as people remain inside their comfort zone, they won't learn anything new that is relevant to behavioral change. Leaning into our discomfort—or as we say, leaning into our blind spot—is necessary to broaden and deepen our awareness, mindset, and skillset. In the age of filter bubbles and cancel culture, the capacity to lean into our discomfort is absolutely critical.

Access Your Non-Action

Always and all the time, focusing on action often leads to *reactive* ways of operating—in other words, doing more of the same but wishing for a different outcome. In the face of a challenge, instead of reacting habitually, actualizing the potential of the emerging future requires developing the capacity to pause and lean into non-action—what we often call our sources of stillness—to allow new knowing and new forms of action to emerge.

Our Zambian colleague Martin Kalungu-Banda taught us about "leading from the gap," and he cites the example of Nelson Mandela. In 1993, Chris Hani, who many considered Mandela's successor, was assassinated. When Mandela received this message, instead of showing anger, he stopped what he was doing and became silent. He was silent for so long that his team began to fear that he might have had a stroke. But then Mandela addressed the nation of South Africa in a historic speech that saved the country from riots and a possible civil war.

> Tonight, I am reaching out to every single South African, black and white, from the very depths of my being. A white man, full of prejudice and hate, came to our country and committed a deed so foul that our whole nation now teeters on the brink of disaster. A white woman, of Afrikaner origin, risked her life so that we may know, and bring to justice, this assassin. The cold-blooded murder of Chris Hani has sent shock waves throughout the country and the world. . . . Now is the time for all South Africans to stand together against those who, from any quarter, wish to destroy what Chris Hani gave his life for—the freedom of all of us.[7]

Mandela was able to transform the very real possibility of seeing his country sink into violence by connecting to an interior space that enabled the country to see itself. Instead of reacting destructively, he paused and stayed with the moment in a space of non-action.

Compare that response with the Bush–Cheney administration's "War on Terror" in reactive response to the terrorist attacks of September 11, 2001. Fast-forward twenty years and you see the enormous costs that those leaders' actions led to:

• The war cost approximately $8 trillion and over nine hundred thousand human lives (these are just the lives lost from "direct war violence"—the total loss of life in post–9/11 war zones is much higher).[8] It also left the

Taliban and Al-Qaeda much stronger than they were before 9/11. And it inspired the creation of ISIS, a terror group much worse than the other two.

- It led to the United States using torture on terrorism suspects, including innocent people, which violated the very values that the war was supposed to defend, and resulted in a comprehensive domestic surveillance system that was previously unthinkable. It sowed mistrust in both domestic and global institutions by moving the United States from a moment of unity and worldwide solidarity to a profoundly different situation shaped by disconnect, mistrust, and anger over the civilian casualties that the war inflicted, particularly on the Muslim world.

- It prompted us to lose sight of the bigger global challenges of our time: our planetary emergency and our self-destructive patterns of polarization.

The capacity to lean into our not-knowing, discomfort, and non-action— or its absence—can have massive real-world consequences, as the examples of Mandela and Bush–Cheney illustrate. They can be seen as critical gateways into the deeper territory of eco-system leadership.

Stories of Impact and Inspiration

Back to "How is all this going to work?" To answer this question, we invite you to sit back, relax, and enjoy a set of stories that feature some of the relevant experiences that allow us to explore this question. These stories approach our current historical moment from different viewpoints, different cultural narratives. And they set the stage for exploring the intellectual roots that underlie this work.

IDEAS Indonesia and Asia Pacific

In early 2003 at MIT, I (Otto) met Cherie Nursalim, the vice chair of an Indonesian business group, who asked me to participate in a conference in Bali the following year.

The war in Afghanistan was ongoing, and the United States had just invaded Iraq. Terrorists had detonated bombs in Bali, and the US State Department had issued a strong advisory against traveling to Indonesia, the world's largest Muslim country. Despite those warnings, I readily accepted the invitation. The reason was Cherie's sincere desire to help create a positive future for her country and region. Also, the organization she represented, called United in Diversity (UID),[9] had been co-founded by the well-known dissident, peace journalist, and activist Aristides "Tides" Katoppo. After talking to Cherie, I knew I couldn't *not* go.

After the conference in Bali, the conversation turned to what could happen next. I was about to launch a program called ELIAS, a tri-sector global leadership program that would bring together key next-generation leaders from across three sectors—business, government, and civil society, including media and universities—in order to prepare them for the disruptive waves of change that even then were already pretty obvious. We would take them on a one-year action learning journey to the places of most potential and equip them with sensemaking and systems-thinking tools that would allow them to co-sense, co-create, and prototype new approaches by working together across sector boundaries.

Cherie told me that was exactly what she wanted to do in Indonesia and that this type of cross-sector U-based action learning journey could have a positive impact on the evolution of the country in its journey toward sustainable development. We agreed that she would identify three people from Indonesia, one from each sector, who would join the Emerging Leaders Innovate Across Sectors (ELIAS) program and then prototype an Indonesian adaptation of it.

A couple of years later we launched the first cohort called Innovative, Dynamic, Education and Action for Sustainability (IDEAS) Indonesia (the name was suggested by an MIT student team that was helping to get it launched) with thirty-five current and emerging changemakers and leaders from across the sectors, including top-level civil servants in the Ministries of Environment, Finance, and Trade; business executives; key players from environmental and social NGOs; and well-known news and talk show anchors. This vast country, an archipelago with over 17,000 islands and a population of approximately 280 million, is also highly diverse, with over 700 spoken languages.

Frans Sugiarta, one of the co-founders of the program, described IDEAS this way: "The way we designed the learning process is more like a dialogue. It's not like teaching."[10] Dr. Ben Chan, Frans, Shobi Lawalata, and Cherie have co-led this and related projects in the years since then, developing a level of trust and collaboration that has allowed it to thrive.

Fast-forward two decades to the current moment. Here are some examples of what has resulted from their shared intention: Eleven cohorts have completed a yearlong leadership journey and devised cross-sectoral solutions for issues related to sustainable development. These solution prototypes have touched over 1 million people in Indonesia. The IDEAS program expanded to include participants from China, Southeast Asia, East Asia, Oceania, and the Pacific Islands.

Over the years, we have seen a shift in the relationships among and between individuals and their respective institutions. They are openly collaborating on initiatives to make their countries more sustainable, inclusive, and aware. These initiatives include domestically replicating action learning and leadership infrastructures for multisector initiatives such as the Just Energy Transition Partnership (JET-P) for transitioning from coal to renewable energy systems, as well as numerous action learning programs for public sector financial institutions, for universities, and for the top echelons of civil servants.

Frans explained some of their success: "At first it was a prototype, and it evolved from one IDEAS group to another. Many prototypes. Then it got replicated across institutions. And then, at some point, it [became] a national policy."[11] The domestic replication was done with minimal external support. Among the prototypes was a project on forest stewardship that acknowledges the rights of Indigenous peoples to ancestral lands and benefits communities living in state forests. Today, Indonesia's national social forestry policy protects Indigenous communities who have lived in state forests for hundreds of years, even before Indonesia existed, who in turn protect the forests.

Another factor that made the whole process feel quite natural and organic over the years was the resonance and alignment between Theory U and some of the core Balinese traditional teachings like *Tri Hita Karana*. Balinese culture is rooted in Hinduism, reflecting the island's spiritual heritage. Tri Hita Karana articulates the three causes of happiness as

- harmony with God, which includes religious and spiritual practices;
- harmony among people, focusing on community and social interactions; and
- harmony with nature, emphasizing environmental stewardship and sustainable practices.

These tenets, grounded in the wisdom of ancient Balinese teachings, resonate with the three divides that Theory U is designed to bridge: the ecological, the social, and the spiritual divides.

Ecosystem Leadership Program (ELP) Latin America

San Esteban, Chile, March 2024. Two hundred and seventy changemakers from seventeen of the nineteen Latin American countries, spanning all the sectors and societal layers, from grassroots changemakers, social justice activists, and Indigenous elders to social media influencers, civil servants, senators, business executives, and academics, gathered together. This may well have been the largest and most diverse group that I (Otto) have ever worked with.

An amazing team of volunteers organized this collective effort, which led a community of twenty-eight organizations to join the Ecosystem Leadership Program (ELP) Latin America (LATAM).[12] The purpose of this annual gathering is to give a community of changemakers across Latin America an opportunity to learn from each other, to connect, and to initiate transformational change in collaboration. By its second year, they had already launched fifty-five different prototype initiatives.

The core holding space is anchored in a spiritually diverse holding group together with *abuelas* and *abuelos* (grandmothers and grandfathers)—that is, elders, community and spiritual leaders from Indigenous traditions across Latin America. They participate in the entire program and lead ceremonies at key junctions along the shared journey. This intentional, diverse, multiyear leadership journey is highly experimental. Two years in, we can already say that it has been a highly transformative experience for just about everyone in-volved—it certainly has been for me.

But let's start at the beginning. The ELP LATAM was co-initiated in 2022 by and with our Uruguayan colleague Laura Pastorini, lead for the Presencing Institute's work in Latin America. Laura had previously taken part in the ELP Global Program in 2019, where we had planted the seeds for regional hubs. She, I, and some other colleagues spent a few days in Chile at the invitation of a foundation to explore how the civil society sector in the country could be better supported through shared learning and leadership infrastructures. We conducted a one-day workshop with local leaders from all sectors. When we saw and reflected on how deeply and directly these changemakers connected with Theory U and social arts practices, Laura said, from the core of her being: "You know what? We need these kinds of deep learning spaces in so many places across the continent." Her intuition started a conversation. An hour later we had created a shared intention to go on a multiyear journey with changemakers there and elsewhere in Latin America.

An important additional input for Laura was an interview that she conducted for a UN project with the Indigenous leader Martin Toc. Laura said:

This interview changed my life. Martin was a very important leader of forty-eight Guatemala cantons of Indigenous communities. He said, "You all are talking about the end of the world. And for us, for the Indigenous people, the world is beginning. It's rising. It's a new era, and we are full of hope. And this new rising in the world has a lot to do with this forgotten knowledge of the Indigenous communities. So, you see the world falling apart and dying. And we see it ready to flourish and shine."[13]

This conversation allowed Laura to confront what she described as a deep wound:

My motivation for this work and for the ELP that could honor ancestral traditions comes from a deep social and personal wound, that makes me feel sad, angry, guilty, and even ashamed because of my skin and my lineage. I was born, grew up in, and live in Uruguay, a country that has no native Indigenous people or culture today. Our Indigenous communities in Uruguay were killed or pushed out as part of the colonization process in the early nineteenth century. And colonization is very much alive today.

She continued:

I began to realize that trying to transform this pain means diving into it, creating the conditions for the system to see, sense, and heal itself. And I think that was mainly why I personally felt the need to do something. . . . How can we transform these wounds into gifts, and how can we make these obstacles, or these structural problems, become resources for transformation? My interview with Martin was the trigger, but then there was a community. I was part of several networks in Latin America that together cultivated the soil for this initiative. I alone could not have done the work. It needed this community of changemakers.[14]

That community of changemakers had met and collaborated in the context of other U-related initiatives before (particularly during the GAIA journey in 2020, an online/offline project that we initiated during the pandemic that created the fertile ground, which we will discuss in more detail in chapter 5).[15] After an intense year of planning, the core team, together with a Brazilian team, launched the ELP LATAM in 2023 just outside of Montevideo. Its 160 participants all brought strong local and regional connections. In the second year the community met just north of Santiago, Chile, at the foot of the Andes for another four-day workshop. Laura reflected, in a conversation with Katrin, on the second gathering:

The first half day was designed so that we could welcome and get to know each other but also clarify the intention for the community. The second day focused on co-sensing. We facilitated a fishbowl process where we brought different voices, mainly from the margins of the system, to the center of the room. This process was also about connecting to our highest potential as leaders, both personally and collectively.

On the third day we had the vision council, a dialogue circle with Indigenous, social, political, and spiritual leaders—about eleven of them stepped on stage. The first four voices of the vision council brought the wound and trauma into the space. I mean, they all came from very complex and violent environments. From the Amazon to the South of Chile, where Indigenous leaders were and still are threatened and killed. They were bringing that anger, that pain, that frustration. They were kind of vomiting this deep wound. . . . Everyone was really struck, and people were crying. I mean, it was a difficult moment. And then they gave the talking stick to Otto, and Otto couldn't speak. He stayed silent and handed the stick to the person on the other side of the stage. That silence was important, it was the empty space at the bottom of the U. And then on the other side there were three of the healers, two medicine women and one medicine man. One of them was really weak, and we were assisting her because she didn't want to leave the stage, she didn't want to leave the circle. . . . And then Amalia, a Mayan medicine woman from Guatemala, entered with beautiful healing words. Then Victor followed. He is a shaman in the Aymara tradition and talked about what was happening in the circle and all around. He said, we need to be aware of what's happening. We are healing on so many dimensions.

Everyone felt this in the room, we felt it in our bodies. We were holding this together. And then Alejandrina from the Peruvian Quechua tradition talked about the beauty and colors of diversity and the healing power of nature. Finally, Miguel, the last one in the circle wrapped up with his eagle view, allowed us to zoom out to understand what was happening. He's a brilliant Indigenous man—a very young man—in his twenties from Arahuacos at the Sierra Nevada in Colombia. The circle ended with Ubiraci from the Brazilian Pataxós, who sang a reconciliation song, that tended a bridge from the stage to the participants, inviting us all to realize that there is no need to be ashamed of our origin or our skin anymore because we are entering a new era of transformation.

After listening to the vision council, we invited everyone to replicate the dialogue round sharing their own vision. At the end each circle wrote a short poem. Every voice was in this poem. This moment in the program felt like we were deeply healing, we all had a sense of healing. You know, it was multidimensional healing. And I felt, well, now I understand why we are here. I felt that everyone was healing their own wound. And we connected to these collective wounds that we were witnessing being healed in real time. I mean, what happened there was profound and totally emergent.

On the last day, when the event had concluded, Otto sat down with Amalia Tum, of the Maya Nation of Guatemala, and Alejandrina Ayala Ninasivincha, from the Aruni-Quechua Nation of Peru—our abuelas, elders, and co-holders of the program. The conversation took place under a tree and was joined and translated by our colleague Sebastian Jung.

Otto opened the conversation by expressing his gratitude and asking them to share their view on the current moment. Alejandrina responded:

The world is made of cycles. Life is going through cycles all the time, isn't it? When the grandparents had the Western presence, it was terrible. They said that they killed us but the roots remained. Then they said that we were going to reproduce like the quinoa. The quinoa seed has more than 1,000 seeds. The Incas have always thought that there are cycles. So, there is a cycle of light, where they flourished in a very short time, they knew that a new century of darkness was coming because in life it is female, male, female, male, etc.

So that is the flourishing of a new era that's coming. What we don't know is who is going to lead that transformation, that new cycle. There are cycles, and the dark cycle, the pacha, lasted for 500 years. That cycle, with all its darkness that we know well, ended in 1992. The new seed was planted in 1992, but it takes time. But this is the time when light is going to appear again. Everything is starting to flourish. It's been over thirty years since 1992. This is the time where the flourishing will start, where the light will start to appear.

Amalia added:

As the grandmother, Alejandrina, says, all cosmovisions are cyclical, just as we humans are cyclical. So, from the Mayan cosmovision we talked about a new dawn, others said it is the end of the world, but in the case of the practitioners directly of Mayan spirituality, we said no, it is not an end of the world, it is a new dawn. And why now? From the Mayan thought we see that this is the moment for the human being to return to his or her environment. Because the earth is crying, screaming, shouting, dancing.

Sebastian observed:

And when, when she was saying the Earth is crying, the horse whinnied loudly just at that moment.

Amalia smiled and continued:

So it's a moment to end with any kind of discrimination, hate, or anger among brothers and sisters. Because there is diversity in the colors of humanity, the colors of the Mayan cosmovision. Red [pointing at the red part of her bracelet] is the color of the new dawn, but it's the color of some human beings—the red brothers. And black [pointing at the bracelet again] represents our black brothers. This [pointing] represents our brothers that have yellow skin. And white is the color of our white brothers, the gringos. That's why we say we're all brothers and sisters. So, when we say we need to listen, it's because we need to feel part of that humanity, to that all human beings belong. Because we are all part of what's being born.

For me, Theory U, for these days here together, has awakened the spirituality, the essence, the heart of those people who are just running, running, running. It is telling us to stop. Live your life in the present moment . . .

Alejandrina responded:

From the northern pole to the southern pole, we are all brothers and sisters. And we share the same consciousness, love, and respect for all cosmic fathers and cosmic mothers. When I meet, for example, the Cherokee people or other Indigenous brothers from the North, we meet ourselves and we feel immediately like brothers and sister. We may argue, we may have different opinions, but we are totally close, and we know how to say sorry, or explain why we did something, and that's it. We hug each other and we are brothers and sisters. Whether they come from Europe, from Asia, from Africa, we're all brothers and sisters.

Amalia shared:

When I was eighteen, I learned to speak Spanish. So last year in the ELP was the first time studying and learning. I have always been in spiritual events, helping the people. Brother Otto, maybe something happened in your life that made you connect with the Earth. I feel that Theory U is totally complete. As Native people we have our own system of authorities, our own economic system, our way of living, the way we grow the earth, everything. So as Native people we look differently at an imposed system of government, where the authorities are imposed. So, the message I understand from my cosmovision regarding Theory U is that this system of people comes to change the system of governments, political and economic systems. This is my understanding.

They come from a system that has an order, and they have lost the natural (ancestral) order. I feel that in Theory U there are many chapters that are cosmovisions. I feel that the Theory U is what allows us to go from a cosmovision to the system, the governmental system, the system of authorities. Not only in Latin America, but all over the world. In every sector. In my cosmovision, for example, I am the timekeeper. In my case, I work with plants.

The cosmic fathers are here. The sun and the moon are here. The earth is here. That's why we say our body is a shrine. It's a temple. The earth is our body. The water is our blood. Fire is our spirit . . .

Alejandrina added:

. . . and wind is our breath. So, the elements and the essence are the same. We all have water, land, wind, plants, et cetera. The elements are the same. Yeah . . . Theory U is waking up consciousness. And that is what we are here for.

Otto responded:

Yes, we are. I want to end with a story about what I experienced repeatedly in China and Southeast Asia. In China, Daoism, Buddhism, and Confucianism are much stronger than many people think. So, I put up the Theory U slide and let people look at it for a few moments. And then with a few words I share the key ideas and ask them what they think. They look at the slide, look at me, and look at each other, and then they say something like, "Who are you? MIT? Are you a gringo? Or a German? *This* [pointing at the slide] is *our* stuff. That's not Western stuff, right?" Then they say: "Open heart, open mind, open will, that's what Buddhism, Daoism, and Confucianism are about. It's the essence of *our* stuff that you have up there on the screen."

In other words, the core principles of many traditions resonate around the world. While some people say that this resonance increases the further you move away from the West, I would not entirely agree with that. And the reason is that there is more than just *one* West.

Yes, there is the West that everyone knows and appropriately criticizes for its patterns of colonization, extraction, and violence. And then there is another less well-known tradition that most people, including many in the West, don't know about. This more contemplative lineage has many different faces and names, including Meister Eckhart, the heretics, Goethe, Hegel, Emmerson, Thoreau, Husserl, Heidegger, Bohm, Eleanor Rosch, and Francisco Varela. That's the lineage that I feel connected to and am building on.

Alejandrina responded:

That's why this connects with people.

Amalia added:

It is not by chance that you invited us today. The energies are perfect. Events happen at the right time, neither before nor after; everything happens at its precise moment. Thanks to existence. We are so blessed by all the gifts of Mother Nature.

The Paris Agreement on Climate Change

The third story plays out on a global stage. We met Christiana Figueres at various UN-related events. In her role as Executive Secretary of the United Nations Framework Convention on Climate Change (UNFCCC), Christiana was responsible for the international climate change negotiations that resulted in the historic Paris Agreement in 2015. For this achievement she has been credited with forging a new brand of collaborative diplomacy.

Later, reflecting on this process in a conversation with Brother Pháp Hữu and Jo Confino in Plum Village, France, in 2022, Christiana shared her personal journey on the road to the Paris Agreement.[16] In 2013 she was confronted with a family situation that came as a shock.

I was working at the United Nations, I was helping my team, the 500 people at the Climate Secretariat, plus 195 nations to build momentum toward the Paris Agreement. And we were right in the middle of the process. And when I became suicidal, I was just crying myself to sleep every single night for months and months . . . and then getting up in the morning and putting a smile on and going to work.

I remember on Christmas Eve when this became absolutely intolerable, I emailed a good friend of mine who lives in Costa Rica, and I said, "Look, I am really dealing very seriously with suicide, and I need something." He says, "Well, what do you need?" And I said, "Buddhism." Now this is in Spanish that I'm communicating with him. And he says, "Buddhism, what do you know about Buddhism?" I said, "I have no idea. Nothing, I know nothing." He goes, "So why do you want that?" "I don't know. But can you please help me out because this is really an emergency situation."

And he goes, "So how do you spell Buddhism in English?" Because he wanted to do a Google search. "I don't know. You know, I think it has a double d, maybe it has a double h. I honestly don't know how to spell it." So, in about 10 minutes, he sent me the link to Plum Village. He doesn't know anything about Buddhism either, right? . . . So, I looked it up and I read whatever was on the web page . . . and I said, "Okay, that is exactly what I need. But there is no way that I can make it to France . . . find me something that is close by." Five minutes later he finds a That monastery in Germany . . . 45 minutes from my house. And I said, "I can do that."

I contacted them via email, but on Christmas Eve they're not exactly responsive to emails. They first said they don't have room. Anyway, finally, they found me a room. By the end of the retreat, I was able to go back to work and those feelings were already much, much more transformed. . . . It was such an avenue of peace and calm and healing for me. And then, later on, what I discovered is, it was transformative. Thầy's [Thích Nhất Hạnh's] teachings were transformative also for the negotiation process.

"Two things," recounts Christiana, "were perhaps the most transformational. One was the skill of deep listening." She notes that in the climate negotiations there were 195 participating countries trying to reach agreement on more than 70 issues, and that each had "different and sometimes mutually exclusive positions." At the negotiating table, "nobody really comes to listen."

When I did have to meet with government officials from almost every country in their capital, I made it a . . . practice to ask them questions and listen to the answers instead of preaching to them what I thought needed to be done. [I asked] them questions about their long-term interests, how they saw themselves growing as a nation, many questions that led them to move from their short-term thinking to a much more longer-term and more inclusive thinking. And the more they move into the future, the more there is an overlap and a coincidence of interest. But that you can only do if you're truly listening to what they're saying and then reflecting back to them so that they begin to see the common ground. The art of deep listening was incredibly helpful.

Also important [the second transformative learning] was that the countries of the Global South felt, justifiably, as if they were the victims of the industrial practices of the Global North. The problem with entering a conversation or negotiation as a victim is there's no way you're ever going to agree with anyone on anything because if you perceive yourself as a victim, you are implicitly accusing somebody else of being a perpetrator.

And so it was so interesting for me to see that if I saw myself in my personal life as a victim, there was no way that I could go into my professional work and expect anything other than a victim–perpetrator dynamic because of the principle of *interbeing*, because [with] the energy that I carry into that dynamic . . . I'm only watering the wrong seeds of being a victim or being a perpetrator. Whereas if I can walk in with a different mindset and understand that I am not a victim, that I have the tools to understand myself differently and that others can do so too, these seeds, these feelings, these paradigms, these dynamics actually evolve at the same time and they're all interconnected, even if that's not evident.

And that was such a lesson to me, such a lesson to me to understand, okay, my first responsibility is for me to get out of my victimhood. That's my first responsibility. And otherwise, I cannot expect anyone else to do that. And so that was a bit of pressure on me, right? It's like, "Okay, you better get your little ducks in a row." But I saw it happen. I saw it happen because in the process of me getting out of my own victimhood, then in my conversation with so many other government representatives, I began to see that lift. And I began to see the emergence of a very, very different dynamic.[17]

We invited Christiana to one of our United Nations Development Program Transformational Leadership journeys, which was with the Presencing Institute, and asked her about the personal leadership practices that helped her to cultivate her inner leadership work.

Yes, these inner practices like deep listening and suspension of judgment need to be cultivated so that they become part of our habit energy. I try to choose a time in the day in which I am really focusing on my inner condition. Just being really mindful [of] how am I reacting. Let's look at an example. I live at the beach. I can see people walking up and down. The first thing I see is who is overweight and who is fit. My immediate unfiltered reaction is, why is that person overweight? Immediately the judgment comes in. . . . First, I already judged that the person is overweight. Maybe from their perspective, they are not overweight. That is what they want to be. And why am I picking up that information? Maybe because I judge myself? And what is that judgment about? . . .

Now it is no longer about that person walking up and down the beach. What did that human evoke in me? Now we take information that is outside and take it inside. And begin to work on ourself. And frankly, that is the only thing you can control. I have no influence on any of the people that walk up and down the beach, or people I work with. I have only control over myself. And as I do that, I hone my skill to truly take responsibility for myself. That is the miracle of this . . . as we soften those hard thoughts, judgments, those blaming fingers in ourselves, we actually begin to melt outside.

You are no longer doing that . . . if you are in conversation with a colleague at work that you have internally judged to be too talkative or too silent. . . . If you take it internally, what is the talkative or silent part in me? The miracle is you begin to see the change in the other person . . . that is the miracle dimension of life, but it does happen. I just invite you to play with that little miracle [for] your own well-being.[18]

So how does Christiana Figueres, arguably one of the most inspiring leaders of our time, actually lead? Here is one way of framing it: by *paying attention to what happens both above and below the surface soil.* She does this in her interpersonal leadership (deepening her listening) and in her strategic leadership, in which she blends formal (top-down) stakeholder relationships with a bottom-up strategy called "operation groundswell" that motivates grassroots activists, academic thought leaders, and other civil society voices.

In our view, all major eco-system leadership challenges require us to deploy both of these strategies that Christiana so masterfully blends: social systems and social soil.

Movement Making: Some Lessons Learned

What do these stories of systems transformation and systems have in common? They share a few key learning experiences that we have also seen in other case stories such as u-lab. Here are five observations and themes that we see emerging across all these stories.

1. If you want to go fast, first you need to go slow.

Everyone talks about needing to speed up. Yet what we have learned is this: to go fast, you first need to go slow. You must do this to cultivate the necessary "soil" conditions, and to ground yourself and your initiative in the power of intention. The whole process of "going down" the U is about just that, slowing down. Slowing down means deepening your attention, decentering your gaze from a mono- to a multicentric view, and inverting your understanding of a situation from a "bubble" mode (stuck in a single echo chamber) to an "eco-field" mode, which allows you to sense a situation from multiple surrounding perspectives.

This principle is embodied in all the stories above, as well as in u-lab: the intention was there long before any opportunity or plan.

2. If you want to go broad, first you need to go deep.

All big things start small. The key to achieving a broader reach is to first focus on building small islands of coherence that, when connected with one another, have the capacity to lift the system. In IDEAS and in the ELP, much of the whole work is in small groups. In u-lab we also apply this principle. We had been working and experimenting with various small local partners that networked and started to co-host and co-activate parts of the global u-lab hub host network.

In other cases it may mean starting small, learning by doing, and then linking up with the larger eco-system. Never underestimate the power of small beginnings.

3. If you want to transform the system, first you need to know yourself.

Personal transformation—as paradoxical as it may sound—is a primary gateway into systems transformation. "The most personal is the most systemic" is how our colleague and friend Peter Senge likes to put it. Christiana Figueres's account of inner leadership work is a powerful example. The same applies to the other stories shared above. Even though traditional approaches to change differentiate between systems and the self, in Theory U the whole point is that the levels are separate *only* when seen through the traditional lens of consciousness (subject-object awareness). But the more we progress toward the deeper levels of awareness—or the bottom of the U—the more these boundaries begin to open up, intertwine, and eventually collapse. In practice, using personal transformation as a gateway to systems change means that the individual cultivation of the social soil has a direct impact on the larger social field.

In u-lab we work on strengthening the self as a key entry point for activating agency. If it is true that the individual and the whole system are inside each other rather than separate from each other, then the inner cultivation work that I engage in is not just my private business. Our individual and shared inner work is, to use an old phrase, "political"; or, to use a more recent term, part of the "commons" that we all have a responsibility to co-cultivate. U-lab methods of strengthening personal transformation as the gateway to systems change include check-ins, presencing practices, case clinics, and prototype clinics. The bottom line of this principle is that if you want to be a good changemaker or leader, you first need to know yourself.

4. If you want to know yourself, first you need to engage with the world.

How do you deepen your self-knowledge? By reflecting on just yourself? No. By going out into the world and by engaging with it *more deeply*. By going to the places of most potential. By relating to the people around you more deeply. Everything that we know about ourselves is sourced through the eyes of others and through their sharing their experiences and views with us. This is very evident in Christiana's story. It's equally evident in the ELP and IDEAS stories. All u-lab methods are grounded in engaging with the world ever more deeply.

5. To profoundly engage with the world, you need to access your emerging self as an instrument for deep knowing.

Very often we see initiatives for change where the actual results do not match the declared goals or intentions. What we have learned over the years is this: unless on that journey there is a collective moment of letting go, a moment of crossing a threshold to a new sense of presence and possibility, it is unlikely that any deeper or profound change will manifest. We believe that crossing this threshold of letting go and letting come establishes a link to a deeper form of collective self-knowing—knowing who we are, why we are here, and what we are here for: the deeper source knowing of the field. This is what we, with our colleague Eva Pomeroy, have started to call fourth-person knowing.[19]

Fourth-person knowing connects to the bottom of the U (see Color Plate 1) and is not merely objective or subjective or intersubjective. Instead, it has a bit of each of those things, plus some additional characteristics that are different from any of the other types of knowledge. For that reason, we refer to it as trans-subjective or self-transcending knowing.

Here are some of the characteristics of fourth-person knowing:

Through me: Fourth-person knowing is deeply personal and is experienced as something that isn't in me but that depends on me to manifest.

When we work with founders of organizations or leadership teams, we often ask them reflection questions such as: *If your organization were a living being that could speak, what would it be saying to you now?* Most founders, CEOs, and team members land on surprisingly meaningful answers. We think it's because they already have a close intuitive relationship with the "beingness" of their organization. Beingness refers to a subtle form of knowing that is different from objective, subjective, or intersubjective knowledge.

Decentering: Fourth-person knowing shows up in our experience through a distinct mode of decentering our perception (i.e., a shift in the experience of space, time, self, light, sensation, and warmth).

This decentering experience is a well-known phenomenon that has been described in experiences of flow,[20] such as when athletes are playing "in the zone,"[21] or when in group processes you enter the bottom of the U. It shows up as *time* slowing down, *space* opening up, a thickening of the *sensual* perception of light. The sense of *self* "decenters" from a single point to a 360-degree sphere of awareness. Often it is accompanied by a felt sense of *warmth* or warm light.

> **Agency:** Fourth-person knowing comes with a heightened sense of possibility in which a future potential that was previously experienced as out of reach suddenly moves inside the horizon of what's possible and doable.

Fourth-person knowing strengthens action confidence and agency. It almost always comes with a heightened sense of capacity to make something that previously felt distant and out of reach a reality. It functions as a gateway for the activation of deep human creativity: the capacity to bring forth realities that previously were not thought possible.

> **Wholeness and freedom:** Fourth-person knowing manifests with an enhanced presence of the whole in individual awareness and of the individual in the shared awareness of a group or a whole.

The result is the possibility for more flexible, loosely coupled organizational structures that operate with higher degrees of freedom to align attention, intention, and agency across all levels, upward and downward. All new flexible forms of organizing and structuring move in the direction of greater local autonomy while maintaining alignment and some coordination on the level of the whole (be that an organization, a region, a country, a continent, or our planet). The trick for successful structural decentralization is an inner alignment around a shared intention of the whole group, distributed throughout the organization. In other words, the deepened sense of alignment that comes with fourth-person knowing is *key* for all current and future forms of fluid, flexible, and decentralized organizing.

In the words of Eva Pomeroy: "Seeing oneself and one's life and work through the lens of the whole is what allows us to align inner intention to shared intention. And there is agency and choice around whether or not to align."[22]

All decentralized autonomous organizations (DAOs) are designed to evolve organically with rapidly changing environments, and to function well they require this deep layer of shared awareness of the whole.

> **Impact:** Fourth-person knowing activates generative social fields and therefore often manifests in sustained, long-term practical results.

Awareness-based knowing can be, in the words of cognitive psychologist Eleanor Rosch, "shockingly effective"[23] because it activates a spark or an inner flame, a generative social field that doesn't fade over time but keeps regenerating itself. That generative field, once activated, produces a continuous stream of loving support, positive energy, practical help, and fresh ideas and initiatives that, if not tossed out after the testing, achieve wider use throughout the larger system.

In summary, the fourth-person view represents a more holistic worldview that is inclusive of the social soil. Actions are weighed not just against human considerations but also against the well-being of all the other beings that humans are co-dependent and co-arising with.

In the age of AI the distinction between fourth-person knowing and traditional forms of knowledge (which our current institutions of learning are organized around) will be ever more important, for obvious reasons: AI will continue to exceed human beings' ability to access and simulate large parts of our first-, second-, and third-person knowledge.

But fourth-person knowing will continue to reside with human beings because this type of knowing—tapping into the future that stays in need of us—is squarely in AI's blind spot. It's the one thing that AI structurally can't do. Fourth-person knowing requires a vehicle that AI does not possess: a knowing sourced through the intelligence of the heart.

To put this evolution in our knowing and thinking into its broadest context, let's turn to the German philosopher Karl Jaspers. He coined the term "axial age" to name a period that ran from roughly 800 to 200 BCE.[24] It referred to the short period of a few centuries during which a whole range of foundational philosophical, intellectual, and religious traditions emerged in China, India, Persia, Judea, and Greece, giving rise to Confucianism, Buddhism, Zoroastrianism, Judaism, and pre-Socratic and Socratic Greek philosophy, during which Plato and Aristotle were active.

While those few centuries that began some 2,800 years ago gave rise to major intellectual approaches that emphasize rationality, ethics, and the nature of reality in the form of different cultural traditions, one way of looking at the current moment is to consider it the beginning of a potential new axial period. If this is the case, it would likely be shaped by some of the key twenty-first-century conditions that we are facing now, including

- the rise of *science*, including quantum physics and AI, which provides a more complex view of the interdependent nature of reality that we co-enact;
- the rise of the planetary *polycrisis* that requires unprecedented levels of collaboration at a planetary level; and
- the emergence of a new *planetary consciousness* that encompasses an astonishing number of people who wish they could be part of a different story of the future.

We all know that the twenty-first-century polycrisis cannot be solved with the same thinking that created it—as Einstein's famous dictum goes. It calls for a major shift or extension of our assumptions:

- *non-reductionist ways of knowing* ("epistemologies") combining traditional data-driven science with other approaches, including systems thinking and phenomenological approaches to science that upgrade our toolkit of not-knowing;

- *holistic approaches to reality* that embrace the full complexity of the inter-beingness of all life forms, systems, and Indigenous ways of knowing; and
- *transdisciplinary approaches* that address the core challenges facing our planet by linking and blending approaches and methods across disciplines, including in the natural sciences, social sciences, humanities, social arts, and Indigenous knowledge systems.

What is fueling all these integrative efforts and developments across separate traditions is a practical need: the convening of very diverse groups with different cultural and knowledge backgrounds described in all of the stories above requires, to be successful, a better support structure. And at the heart of that support structure, we need a more holistic and integrative scientific methodology.

Throughout all these efforts we see integrative efforts emerging that cut across various forms of knowing:

neuroscience, neurophenomenology: Varela, Rosch and Thompson,[25] Petitmengin,[26] Rosch,[27] Valenzuela-Moguillansky[28]

Eastern/Asian epistemologies: Huai-Chin[29] (Daoism, Buddhism, Confucianism)

Indigenous ways of knowing: Goodchild,[30] Yunkaporta,[31] Kimmerer[32]

Ubuntu and African epistemologies: Akómoláfé,[33] Kalungu-Banda[34]

social arts and aesthetic ways of knowing: Hayashi and Dutra,[35] Bird[36]

applications of mindfulness in health and education: mindfulness-based stress reduction (MBSR);[37] social-emotional learning[38]

leadership and systems change: awareness-based systems change[39]

praxis-based ways of knowing: Scharmer and Pomeroy,[40] Schein,[41] contributors to the *Journal of Awareness-Based Systems Change*

holistic Western epistemologies: work of Goethe,[42] Husserl,[43] Maturana and Varela,[44] Meadows, Randers, and Meadows,[45] Zajonc,[46] and Senge[47]

How do these different roots, lineages, and practice fields flow together to form a larger river, or, in the language of Dr. Melanie Goodchild, the peaceful and mutually respectful coexistence that is exemplified by the Two-Row Wampum Belt, highlighting the ethical relational space that emerges *between* distinct epistemologies?[48]

The process of engaging in this ethical space is something Melanie has termed *relational systems thinking*, "where awareness-based systems change centers *mutual benefit* . . . between all the humans, the non-humans, the unborn generations and our Earth Mother."[49]

This ethical relational space and our ways of connecting and integrating matter because they are essential for practical movement building. We started this chapter by asking, *How can we make visible the invisible side of transformation— the social soil—and make it more methodically accessible for our inquiry and understanding?* The concept of fourth-person knowing represents a step into this more holistic and integrative space of emergence that, as Goodchild proposes, "is *mashkiki* (medicine) and that inviting the medicine to flow in the space between worldviews is healing. It is letting the medicine flow at the interface where two bodies of water come together."[50]

Presencing versus Absencing: A Divide Running through Our Hearts

Let us conclude this middle chapter of the book by contemplating the intertwined relationship between presencing and absencing. They may seem like hard opposites, but that simple view does not get to heart of the matter.

In fact, presencing is not the opposite of absencing. It's the middle way. Let us explain.

A good starting point is to consider how we respond to disruptions. Figure 4.2 depicts presencing and absencing as two of three options; the third is to continue with doing more of the same, a process we will call *downloading*.

When we face a disruptive situation, we can respond by doing more of the same (downloading), turning away and closing down (absencing), or turning toward the disruption and opening up (presencing).

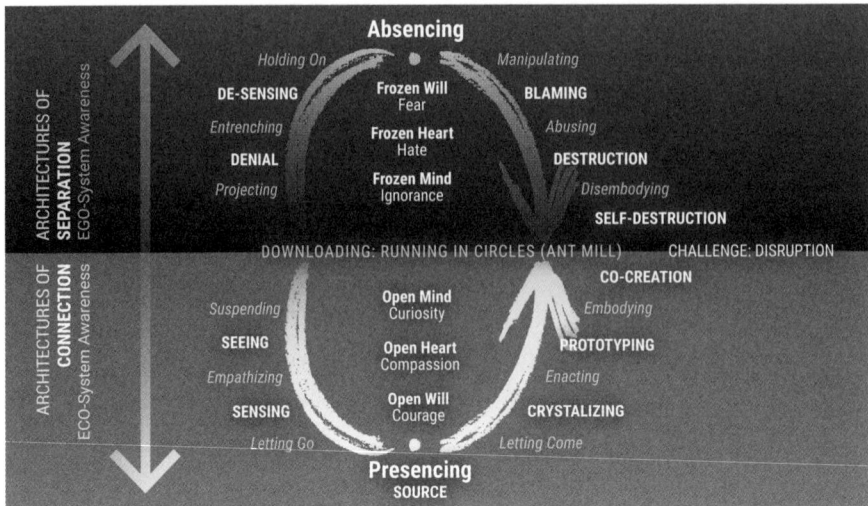

FIGURE 4.2: DOWNLOADING, PRESENCING, AND ABSENCING: THREE MODES OF RESPONDING TO DISRUPTION

Downloading: doing "more of the same," what Báyò Akómoláfé, the Nigerian philosopher and poet, describes as *running in circles*, is a type of behavior reminiscent of ants in ant mills—a phenomenon in which army ants chase each other in a circle, endlessly, until they finally die of exhaustion.

Turning backward: trying to make something (a past period) "great again"—a phrase that we have heard echo across geographies over the past decade or so.

Turning forward: turning toward the challenge of the larger system by leaning in, co-sensing and co-creating a more inclusive outcome.

Otto first presented this image toward the end of the book *Theory U* in 2006.

I introduced the idea of absencing as a cycle of destruction and eventual self-destruction. The obvious example for me, as a German American who grew up in Germany, was that of Hitler and Nazi Germany. Twenty years on, in 2025, there is no longer any need to use a twentieth-century example.

Anywhere in the world today, when you show this picture, people immediately know what we are talking about. They look at the graphic and recognize it as something that's happening today in all of the world's regions. And they say, "Yep, that's exactly what we are dealing with now."

Presencing as a Path for Balancing Polarities

For a deeper look at the intertwined relationship between presencing and absencing, see Figure 4.3.

The figure depicts presencing not as the opposite of absencing but as an integrative middle way holding the polarity of two opposing types of absencing: one that is overexpanding and the other is overdiminishing the self.

As Figure 4.3 shows, the open mind can be seen as a middle way between the Voice of Judgment (overexpanding) and Voice of Doubt (overdiminishing).

Likewise, the open heart can be seen as a middle path between the Voice of Hate (overexpanding) and the Voice of Depression (overdiminishing); and the open will can be seen as a middle path between the Voice of Fanaticism (overexpanding) and the Voice of Fear (overdiminishing).

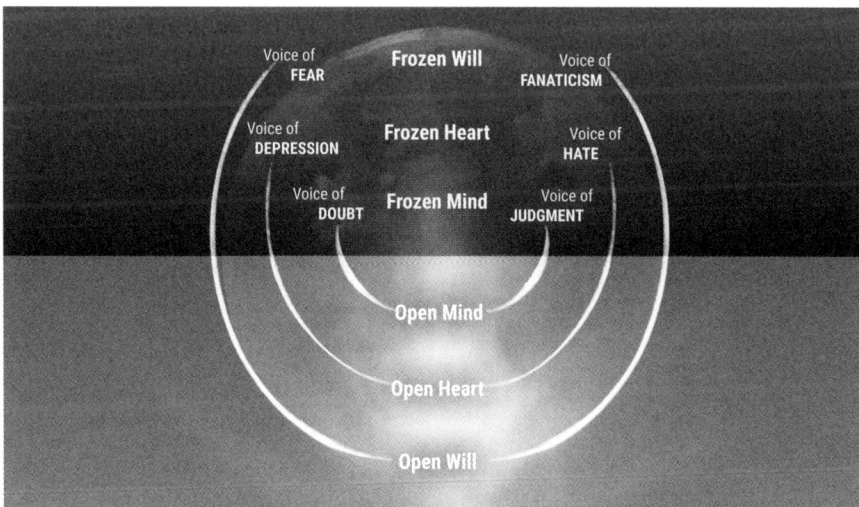

FIGURE 4.3: PRESENCING AS BALANCING THE EXTREMES OF ABSENCING

Presencing is neither one extreme nor the other. Presencing is about holding the space for the middle path where these polarities can be integrated.

In other words, absencing comes in two different types: one that overexpands and one that overdiminishes the presence of self through hubris or self-denial, respectively. In both cases there is a loss of a same-level interpersonal relationship. In the case of the *overdiminishing or self-denying the self,* we end up in a place of doubt, depression, and fear that puts us into a state of *perpetual self-paralysis.*

In the case of the overexpanded self, we end up in a place of judgment, hate, and rigidity (or fanaticism) that puts us into a state of *self-aggrandizing hubris* and *aggressive overreach.*

Presencing deals with the same set of forces and polarities that absencing does, but from a different inner intention and place. That place is about humbly holding a middle path that helps us not deviate into the landscape of self-denying paralysis or aggressive overreach.

In other words, the boundary between presencing and absencing is not a boundary that separates one group of people from the other. That boundary is a thin line that runs right through, in the words of Joanna Macy, "the landscape of our hearts."[51]

Advancing through that middle way helps us to establish a more balanced and harmonious web of relationships. While all six forms of absencing operate on a steep self–other gradient that puts one's self *above* others in one case (superiority complex) or *beneath* them in the other case (inferiority complex), the pathway to presencing calls for holding the possibility of integrating these polarities rather than using them as fuel for polarization.

The middle way is of course in many ways reminiscent of the Tao in Daoism.

The Tao of U

Daoism is a philosophical and spiritual tradition that has shaped Chinese culture alongside Confucianism and Buddhism. The principles explored in this chapter resonate deeply with the principles in a variety of wisdom traditions, but the above framing of presencing as the middle way and the gateways of not-knowing, discomfort, and not-doing particularly resonate with philosophical principles underlying Daoism.

The Dao is often translated as "the Way." It can be understood as the ultimate source principle from which everything arises and takes shape, and then eventually returns to.

The term *source* in Theory U refers to the sources of our deeper ways of knowing and being, of our creativity, and of our inner knowing, including our "fourth-person" collective self-knowing.

The term *source* in Theory U is a nod to all great wisdom traditions that over the millennia have developed terminologies and practices for establishing these deepened connections. It is also a nod to Daoism in which *source* plays a prominent role, as I have learned over the years from friends and many visits to China.

"The Tao that can be told is not the eternal Tao; the name that can be named is not the eternal name." These famous opening lines of the *Tao Te Ching* by Lao Tzu point to the true nature of the Tao, which cannot be put into words. Daoism, with its Indigenous roots and its emphasis on living in harmony with nature, has long been looked down upon and suppressed. But lately, in the face of our global environmental challenges, it has received renewed interest.

For example, the core principle of yin and yang describes the interdependent complementarity of opposites and is closely related to the discussion of presencing and absencing. The lefthand side of the U, as our Chinese colleague and friend Lili Xu first explained to me, emphasizes the yin—femininity or holding the space. The righthand side of the U emphasizes the yang—masculinity or intentional action. These opposing energies need to be in dynamic harmony in order to co-evolve together.

The principle of *wu wei* refers to the practice of taking no action when it is unnecessary. This principle teaches that true effectiveness in action comes from following the natural currents of events, without exerting effort against the natural order. In other words, *wu wei* is strongly related to the principle of nonaction.

But what, then, is the Tao of the U? In our view, the Tao of the U has to do with the opening lines of this book, the conversation about our current moment: Are we going to sink, or are we going to rise? As we all know, we are living in an existential planetary moment at the bottom of the U, which we can open up to and experience—or numb ourselves against—on all levels of our being.

In our own lives, what we have always found most helpful when facing an existential threshold is the *unconditional confidence* in our capacity to be present and to rise to the occasion. This grounding principle is perhaps nowhere better articulated than in these words: *There is nothing that arises in our experience that we are not big enough to hold.*

These words by our South African colleague Marian Goodman ring true because they resonate with our own experience and being; they express an unconditional trust and confidence in what exists now and what is about to emerge. It is that unconditional trust and confidence that we can tap into to reshape our relationship to others, to ourselves, and to the universe. Without unconditional trust and confidence, nothing profoundly new can happen that is a force for good. Without deep trust we will likely end up doing more of the same—running in circles. But what is the ultimate source of that confidence and trust? It is the belief and experience that we are not alone. We are in this together.

Gateways

We opened this chapter by asking how to make the deep structures of systems change visible. In exploring that question, we discussed Varela's claim that there is a blind spot in Western science regarding how we access experience. And after diving into some stories of change, we explored the knowledge and knowing that it takes to cope with today's profound challenges in our workplaces, in our societies, and in our communities. All of that led us to fourth-person knowing: the deep self-knowing of the field.

But when we *are* in the face of absencing, how can we hold the middle way? Are we really big enough to hold the enormous tensions that in the age of hyperpolarization and increased trauma and violence are coming our way? When we find ourselves in the midst of absencing, what exactly is ours to do?

Our colleague Eva Pomeroy names as conditions for holding the middle way the capacity "to connect to a deeper purpose, to trust that what we do matters" and, most importantly, to be confident that "we are not alone."[52]

All this brings us back to the notion of the three gateways to or access points of our deeper sources of knowing. They are visualized in Figure 4.4 in terms of how they related to absencing and presencing, and how they allow us to move from one to the other:

- access your not-knowing by activating your "humble listening;"[53]
- access your discomfort by activating your sensing, empathy, and love; and
- access your non-action by activating your letting go stillness and presencing.

The root of the word presencing is *es*, which means "to be"—that is, "I am." *Essence, yes, presence,* and *present* (gift) all share this same Indo-European root. An Old Indian derivative of this same root from India is *sat*, which means both "truth" and "goodness." This term became a major force in the twentieth century, when Mahatma Gandhi used it to convey his key notion of *satyagraha* (his strategy of truth and nonviolence). An Old German derivative from

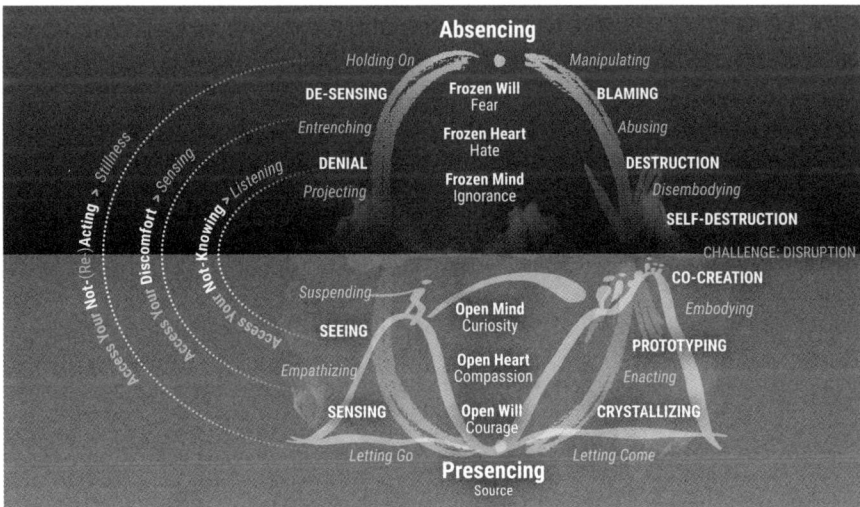

FIGURE 4.4: THREE GATEWAYS TO DEEPER KNOWING

the same root, *sun*, means "those who are surrounding us" or "the beings who surround us."

Contemplating this, Otto reflects:

As I write these lines I am just returning from my father's funeral in Germany. He was ninety-four and had a blessed life. My siblings and I were blessed to be with him during his final few days, hours, and moments. When you approach the crossing of the threshold of death by a loved one, what is it that you experience? You experience an extreme form of not-knowing, of discomfort, and of non-action. When all the medical interventions have run their course, what's left is your *presence* and your *love* for each other—just being with what is about to happen, holding the space.

In these special moments, as Marian Goodman put it, the veil between the physical and the spiritual worlds gets thinner and more permeable. To me it felt as if that veil, in the end, got so thin that it finally floated away in the moment of passing. During the wake on the farm, when my father's many fellow travelers from decades past arrived to say their goodbyes, the veil stayed very thin for three more days. On the third day, during the ceremony that marked his final departure from the farm, as his grandchildren carried him out, we could hear the farm animals voicing their goodbyes: first a cow, then a rooster, and finally a dove. When the car with his coffin drove silently down the farm's 0.8 km driveway, we could sense the lifting of the veil between him and the *eco-system being* of the farm—all the plants, animals, and people who reside and thrive together on that little piece of earth.

Chapter 5

Eco-system Leadership

Seven Practices for Cultivating the Social Soil

Our calling is to serve the cultivation [Bildung] of the Earth.
—NOVALIS

My father loved this quote from the eighteenth-century writer and philosopher Novalis. In the German original, Novalis uses the word *Bildung*. Bildung is a German word for a tradition of self-cultivation that links philosophy and education to the process of achieving full human actualization. Bildung has also gained some recognition in the English-speaking world through the book *The Nordic Secret*.[1] The book's authors suggest that the success of the European Nordic countries—which top most of the international rankings in outcomes for health, learning, and government efficiency—can be attributed to the Danish Folk High School, which, starting in the 1840s, adopted a holistic educational model inspired by the concept of Bildung. Once the rest of the Nordic countries adopted this educational model, argue the authors, within a decade the economic and social development in these countries began to take off.

Six months before his death, my father gave a speech to 1,000 fellow regenerative farmers from around the world in Switzerland. As he prepared that speech, I helped him to reflect on the critical turning points in his life. Two of them stood out. One was that, as a young farmer in his mid-twenties, one morning he saw five dead cows in an area of his land where he knew that some agricultural research experiments had taken place. He realized that the underlying approach of industrial agriculture that he had been taught in school and had practiced since was broken. So he looked for alternatives. A friend gave him a small book on biodynamic agriculture. He was excited about its holistic paradigm, looked at the few farms that had been pioneering this approach, and decided to go all in.

The other formative experience happened a few years earlier. He attended a Danish Folk High School for one winter. There the students and teachers formed a living community where they had meals and conversations around the same table. On his family's farm, he had grown up with one table for his family and another one for the workers. Throughout his childhood, my father much preferred to hang out with the workers. But only when he experienced the shared communal space between teachers and students did it dawn on him what an alternative model might look like. When eventually he took over the family farm, he quickly changed the way it operated, choosing to run the farm as a cooperative community.

In his final speech as a ninety-four-year-old in front of 1,000 of his co-pioneers, his closing message was clear and simple: the soil and the community need to be cultivated together. You can't do one without the other. That was the essence of his lived experience.

Which brings us back to Novalis. We are called to serve the cultivation of earth. The use of the word Bildung in the context of earth is evocative, to say the least, and hints at a hidden connection between the cultivation of the soil and the cultivation of our essence, our humanity.

Humus, Humanity, and Humility

With that idea in the back of my mind, it came as no surprise that the etymological origin of *humus, humanity,* and *humility* is the same. The origin of all three is the Indo-European *ghom-*, which means "earth" or "ground." This word root gave rise to a whole range of words related to soil, earth, and land. A connection between humus and humanity might suggest that humans, like humus (organic soil matter), literally originate from and remain rooted to the earth. In a similar context, *humility* suggests closeness to the ground, as opposed to being elevated or arrogant.

Our colleague from Uruguay, Laura Pastorini, told us about a conversation she had with Juven Piranga, a major of the Coreguaje Indigenous community in Colombia. He told her that they believe the final purpose of humans is to become fertilizer for the earth. When someone passes away, they say, "They are now fertilizing the earth." Clearly, this idea connects humanity, humus, and humility to compost, and we are humbled to nourish the earth that nourishes us.[2]

When we introduced the concept of the social field in chapter 2, we described it in binary terms: the visible part exists above the surface of the soil and the invisible below the surface. Now let's think about it from a nonbinary point of view. Viewed more holistically, the layer of topsoil on our planet and the social soil in our societal systems do not exist in isolation. They exist and come into being as a *mediating membrane* between different worlds or spheres of being, which they relate to and connect, while giving rise to a new world that would not otherwise exist.

Soil, organic matter, is created by the connection between the atmosphere and the lithosphere and functions as a mediating membrane that allows the two spheres to interact through processes like climate regulation, water retention, and nutrient cycling. Soil and water are essential for the entire *biosphere* to rise and flourish.

Likewise, *attention* arises from the connection between the visible exterior of social systems (actions and words) and the invisible interior (thoughts, feelings, intentions). Attention functions as a mediating membrane that allows the two realms to interact through processes like empathic listening, dialogue, teamwork, and shared governance. Attention, if cultivated, is the foundation that makes it possible for the entire *social sphere* to rise and flourish.

We can say that *attention* is to the social field what *humus* or topsoil is to the agricultural field. A good layer of humus is the best indicator of a healthy carbon-capture cycle and a flourishing environmental eco-system. A good amount of shared attention and intention in a social eco-system is the best indicator of social flourishing.

What, then, is the expression of our essence, our humanity? Perhaps, like the essence of humus, it is to live at the cross section of different spheres—of different worlds—to weave and connect them in ways that give rise to new worlds: the biosphere and the social sphere, respectively, and everything that continues to manifest through them. And it is to participate in all of this in the spirit of humility and humanity.

Eco-system Leadership

Eco-system leadership focuses on the *Bildung* of the earth soil and the social soil. Just as the farmer relies on practical tools such as the chisel plow to nourish and cultivate that thin layer of topsoil, the farmers of the *social field*—which is each and every one of us—also require effective tools to deepen the quality of attention, intention, and relationships. The seven practices described in this chapter depict seven critical capacities of eco-system leadership. If embodied, these practices add up to what we call *vertical transformation literacy*: the capacity—in the face of disruption and collapse—to co-sense and co-create the future *as it emerges.*

In chapter 3 we referred to the seven capacities on the lower hemisphere of the Wheel of Deep Change as our dormant superpowers. We all have the seeds of these superpowers within us. But in order to sprout and thrive, these seeds need high-quality soil. The seven practices described in this chapter will help you cultivate that soil so the seeds can grow to their fullest potential. We also provide tools and exercises that support the application of these practices. For more detail and other tools and resources, visit u-school.org/.

The seven practices of eco-system leadership are straightforward. Some will be familiar to you, and some less so. Each of us can cultivate the practices in our own lives. In doing so, we will co-shape the foundations for the larger shifts that our planetary moment is calling for.

The upper half of Foldout Color Plate 1 visualizes shifts on the systems level; the lower half presents seven enabling leadership practices. The progression from the outer (OS 1.0 and 2.0) to the inner spheres (3.0 and 4.0) tracks which kinds of systemic shifts require which advancements in leadership practices.

Eco-system leadership is characterized by

- multiple centers of leadership (it is multipolar, not unipolar);
- integrating of polarities, rather than fragmentation through polarization; and
- dynamic evolution from current to future states, rather than "stuckness" in patterns of the past.

In essence, eco-system leadership is the capacity to align attention, intention, and agency at the level of the whole. How does one acquire this capacity? By cultivating these seven practices throughout the system.

Eco-system leadership is not needed everywhere. For example, in situations of low complexity it is usually not necessary. But when systems face disruptive challenges and need to reimagine and reshape themselves, eco-system leadership and its seven core practices can be transformative.

Practice 1: Becoming Aware—Bending the Beam of Attention Back onto Ourselves

Just as the functional equivalent of humus in a social field is *attention*, the process of "becoming aware" is foundational for the cultivation of the social soil. And just as the plow turns, opens, and cultivates the surface of the soil, the turning and bending of the beam of attention cultivates the *social soil* by opening up the minds, hearts, and wills of the participants in a system.

The quality of our attention shapes the quality of our individual and collective actions, just as the quality of the Earth's soil determines the quality of the harvest. How we pay attention and what we pay attention to matters.

In a time when both our soil and our attention have become the primary targets of extractive, multibillion-dollar industries—Big Ag and Big Tech—*regaining control* of our soil through regenerative agriculture and of our attention through awareness practices are imperatives for all future development. We will not create a regenerative society without regaining control of both our attention and our soil, in the sense of independence from highly extractive business models that drive major parts of our Big Ag and Big Tech industries.

The research that led to earlier iterations of our work on Theory U includes comprehensive interviews with entrepreneurs, changemakers, cognitive scientists, and other innovators on the question of how to connect to an emerging future and bring this potential into the world. In one interview, Bill O'Brien, the late CEO of Hanover Insurance, who led transformational change processes there for many years, summarized what he had learned with a simple observation: "The success of an intervention depends on the *interior condition* of the intervenor."[3] How we show up, our interior condition, the quality of presence, attention, and intention that we bring to the present moment, matters. It shapes the quality of our relationships, which in turn creates practical results.

Paying Attention to Your Attention

Most of the time we tend to focus our attention on things that are outside of ourselves. *Paying attention to our attention* invites us to do the opposite: to bend the beam of attention back onto its own process and source. The source can be an individual or a group, an organization or the society we live in. But it all starts with *paying attention to our attention.*

Consider this. When you throw a stick in front of a dog, the dog always goes after the stick. When you throw the same stick in front of a lion, the lion *turns his head* to see where the stick came from, *directly looking at YOU.* While the dog is always chasing the object, the lion redirects his attention from the object to the source.[4]

How often, in organizations and in society, do we respond to situations the way the dog does? How often do we respond to situations the way the lion does? When life throws the next stick in front of you—in the form of a new message on your device or a disruption of some sort, or in the form of an incentive that someone dangles in front of you—what do you do? Do you react like a dog, automatically chasing after the object? Or do you respond like a lion, by accessing stillness and turning your attention from the object to the source?

Our systems of communication and public discourse are designed to grab our attention, not to invite us to contemplate our options. The platforms on our electronic devices are intentionally designed to keep us stuck in reactive loops. They target and exploit our personal vulnerabilities to maximize user engagement, often by triggering anger, hate, or fear. The social media industry is a trillion-dollar industry *because its tactics work.* Using data analytics to convert our experience to information that makes us manipulable has been a winning proposition for some companies—and a losing proposition for society and humanity.

Eileen Fisher, the founder of a sustainable fashion brand, reflects on the role of aligning *attention* and *intention* in leadership:

> I think change starts from within. I believe we all have a purpose in life, even if we don't know what it is yet. Sometimes it emerges as we are just trying to show up and be present in our lives. Self-reflection and mindfulness have helped me do this. For instance, the moment of silence we take before meetings at the company. It gives me the opportunity to stop and just notice what's actually presenting itself in front of me. . . . What matters is how each of us shows up and brings our unique voice into the moment. . . . It's about finding your voice, knowing that it matters, and having the confidence to share it."[5]

Paying attention to our attention can happen in many ways. At Eileen Fisher every meeting begins with a moment of silence during which the team can start to pay attention to their attention. This moment invites team members to connect to the intention they hold and bring it into the meeting.

Bending the beam of attention back onto yourself requires *stopping doing what you're doing habitually* and *becoming aware of yourself* in the context that you are operating in. You shift your *ego*-perspective (sourced from a single perspective inside your bubble) to an *eco*-perspective (sourced from multiple perspectives beyond your bubble). Doing so does not mean giving up who you are but rather *extending your awareness* of who you are, and who we are.

Bending the beam of attention back onto ourselves gives us the power and opportunity to *transform old patterns* of producing results that no one wants. By (re)aligning *attention* and *intention*, we generate a field of *coherence* that allows for a future that is different from the past.

This alignment can happen on an individual and a collective level. On a personal level, this alignment enables us to connect to our purpose and sources of emergence. For teams and organizations, it creates trust and ease of collaboration. It can also be generative in larger social fields that we are part of, such as a community, neighborhood, or society.

This shift in attention provides us with new perspectives. But if the bending of the attentional beam is so powerful, why haven't we made use of it more widely? Why, for example, does it go unmentioned in most educational settings? As powerful as it is, it is an inner shift that remains by and large invisible to the eye.

The lack of attention to this practice is the result of us overvaluing the upper half of the Wheel of Deep Change and undervaluing the lower, less visible half of the social field, the social soil. The essence of *becoming aware* is *not* to sit in isolation and ruminate about yourself and the state of the world. On the contrary, the essence of becoming aware is to engage with the world more deeply.

The three gateways (or pathways) for deepening our experience in ways that allow us to eventually bend the beam of attention back are the ones that we referred to earlier:

- accessing not-knowing: humility;
- accessing discomfort: love; and
- accessing not-doing: stillness.

When we do those things, we allow the new to emerge.

Tool: Awareness Practices

Paying attention to our attention and realigning attention and intention are the hallmarks of all forms of awareness practices, from mindfulness exercises to leading processes for teams and groups. Here are two simple tools:

For individuals: Start and end the day with a reflective practice. Like a moment of intentional stillness in the early morning and a bit of journaling or reflection at the end of the day. Think about your actions, your feelings, and your ideas during the day. Look at yourself from the outside. What are you noticing?

For teams: Start and end your meetings with a moment of silence (in the beginning) and a moment of reflection at the end (what worked, what didn't, what are we noticing about our own process?).[6]

Practice 2: Holding the Space Within—Listening with Your Mind and Heart Wide Open

Listening is a straightforward application of bending our attentional beam. The more we bend it, the deeper we listen. Generative listening is the antidote to the filter bubbles and echo chambers that social media forms around us.

Most people think of themselves as good listeners. And most people, when given some reflection tools, quickly realize that their listening is imperfect. That's usually the moment when a journey of deepening our capacity for listening begins. Changing the way we listen sounds like a small thing. But when you change how you listen, you change the quality of your *relationships*, the quality of *your experience*, and the quality of the experiences of those *around* you. And when you change those things, you change, well, *everything*.

Listening as a leadership capacity is often enormously underrated. Listening is a crucial component of leadership and many other advanced professional competencies and skills. If you are not a good listener, you are likely out of touch with reality. And if you are out of touch with reality, you cannot be good at anything. Our colleague Kelvy Bird, who developed the visual art of generative scribing, says this about her own listening as a scribe in meetings and other group settings: "When listening, we attend to the parts, the interdependencies, and the meaning—all at once."[7]

Our colleague Manish Srivastava, who works on complex multistakeholder social change processes in India and elsewhere, talks of how shifting his way of listening affected him:

I was part of a multisectoral partnership of nonprofits, government, business. I was representing Unilever, and we were working on the issue of child malnutrition. We were sitting in a circle, and I remember that the conversation started moving toward the role of women and what could be done to support them. There were experts in the room—doctors and scientists—as well as women from the local communities. The conversation went on for maybe an hour.

Eventually someone noticed a woman who was almost curling up in her chair and asked if she wanted to say something. When all the attention turned to her, she hesitated but then noted that for the past hour only men had spoken. She pointed out that the topic was women, mothers, and children. Everybody became quiet. I felt her comments like a wake-up call. When some women from the village then began to speak, we all listened so intensely that no one thought to switch on the lights when the sun began to set. My assumed privilege as a man made it easy for me to speak up. When my awareness shifted, I saw the blind spot of my privilege. That experience became a reference point for reframing my sense of self and my listening. This moment had an impact on everyone in the meeting. At one point one of the women began to sing a beautiful song about giving rain to the land and giving food to children. That was a shift. After that meeting, the group was committed to collaborate on a different level. We worked together for years, and this group had a huge impact on the health of children in this area. We became such a powerful coalition.[8]

Generative listening is available to everyone. But it takes practice. We have learned that activating generative listening can be a much faster process than most people might think. For example, in a six-week class that Otto teaches at MIT, a group of sixty students from around the world works to transform their level of listening in group meetings and through daily personal practices. And yes, it takes personal intention and a support structure. The support structure consists of tools, practice fields, and community. The three guiding principles for cultivating generative listening are the following:

- access your not-knowing by *suspending your habits of judgment* (open mind);
- access your discomfort and empathy by *redirecting your attention* (open heart); and
- access your not-doing and stillness by *letting go and holding the space* (open will).

Manish said that when he suspended his habits of judgment, he was able to redirect his attention from himself to the women in the room and hold the space for what began to emerge.

Four Levels of Listening

In our work with teams and groups, we have identified different ways and qualities of listening. The following tools help us evaluate our own ways of listening. The distinction between *four levels of listening* enables us to become aware of how we listen and to adapt our quality of listening to what is needed and appropriate in the moment (see Figure 5.1):

- *Downloading* is the mode of listening that most of us use daily out of habit. In most interactions, we download (or hear) what we already know. Nothing new enters our mind. We sit in meetings, talk to our family members, and navigate our daily routines by applying our past experiences to what is happening in front of us. Downloading can be

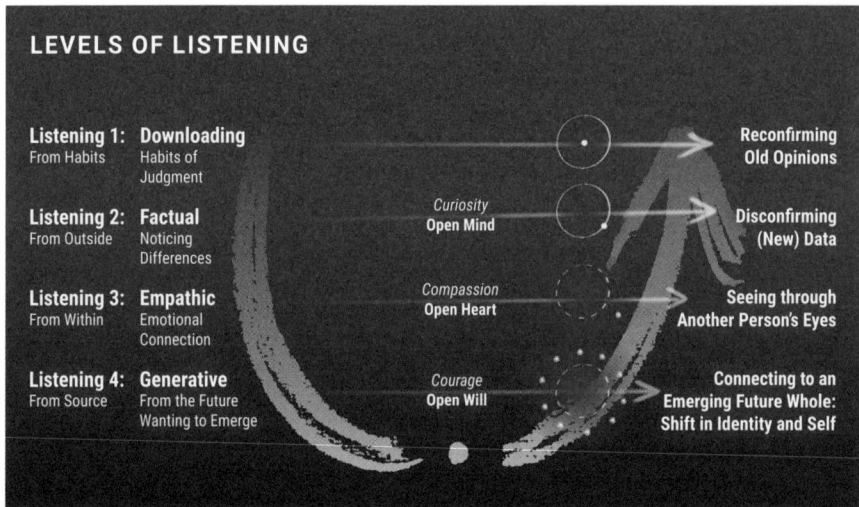

FIGURE 5.1: FOUR LEVELS OF LISTENING

appropriate in many situations. For example, if we find ourselves inside a burning building with others, we want everyone to jump instantly into emergency protocols and routines. But in situations that cannot be responded to adequately with existing habits and protocols, other modes of listening are more useful.

• *Factual listening* focuses my attention on what's surprising or new. I pay attention and notice how it is different from what I had assumed would happen. I lean in with curiosity. Factual listening is the foundation of science: let the data talk to you. Charles Darwin, for example, carried a small notebook to write down disconfirming data that he came across. He knew that our minds tend to disregard observations that do not fit our existing mental frames. Through factual listening we absorb new information with a subject–object consciousness: I am in here, and the world out there is offering me a new piece of information.

• *Empathic listening* moves the focus from "out there" to a more dynamic multiperspective world of lived experience. This mode of listening activates the amazing human ability to step into the perspective of someone else when we use our empathy as an *organ of perception*. We can do that by activating our mirror neurons. Mirror neurons are activated by feelings of empathy for someone other than ourselves. We activate this level of listening by opening our heart and by moving the source of our attention from ourselves to someone else. Although we might not agree with another person, we are able to see the situation from their perspective, *through their* eyes.

- *Generative listening* further expands listening by encompassing the whole social field. The source of our listening moves from what *is* (what has already emerged) to what is about to emerge. It's a flow state that sports teams refer to as playing "in the zone" and musicians refer to as being "in the groove." It's an effortless way of being, sensing, and acting together that makes it feel as if all boundaries have collapsed.

Distinguishing between levels of listening is a conceptual tool that anyone can apply to their own listening. In general, the differences between Levels 1, 2, and 3 are easy to understand; the boundary between Levels 3 and 4 is less obvious. We suggest not focusing on that. For beginners, the most important distinction is that between Levels 1 and 2 (listening from the head), and Level 3 (listening from the heart).

The Practice Field and Community

We use two tools to deepen our level of listening. The first tool is the "empathy walk."[9] In that activity, participants spend a couple of hours with a person who (a) they don't know and (b) is different from them in some important way (class, race, ethnicity, politics, ideology, worldview, or more than one of these dimensions). The practice of deeply and humbly listening to a stranger, developed by the late Ed Schein, takes you outside your own bubble and into someone else's world in an hour or two. Participants then write a one-page reflection on the experience.

The second tool is the Case Clinic,[10] a highly structured process that takes a group through the seven steps of the U-process in one hour. One person presents a case that they are a key player in and in which they could make a big difference in the outcome. The other group members listen with their minds and hearts wide open. The facilitator asks the group to enter stillness, to sense deep resonance, and to mirror their thoughts, feelings, and reflections back to the case giver via gestures and images. This resonance given through images and gestures allows the group to deepen their awareness of the situation and is the entry point for a generative dialogue that, ideally, is profoundly helpful and often transformative for the case giver.

In our work, we aim to democratize access to these spaces for changemakers at all levels, from individuals and small groups to organizations and larger systems. One of these spaces is our free online/offline platform called u-lab. As one of the u-lab participants shared with us: "It has been in these moments of guided stillness where I could suddenly feel that I am not alone. I could feel the connection to all the other changemakers and initiatives around the world. Many of us advance or want to advance similar ideas and initiatives in different systems, contexts, and geographies. Feeling that connection made me finally believe in my own ideas and intentions that I want to move forward now."[11]

Practice 3: Dialogue—Holding Space for Systems to See and Sense Themselves

Conversation is not just another process. It is a *primary* process that generates the world that we—as changemakers, leaders, and human beings—deal with moment to moment. Much of leading change work is about *turning the focus of our attention* from the surface level—*what* is being said—to the deeper layers and structures of *how* and from which *sources* we co-enact conversations in different situations.

Over the past decade or so, in parallel with the rise of social media, the quality of conversation in the public arena has significantly declined. Yet we have also witnessed many new conversations, including citizen-led initiatives and community dialogues. One example of a business-led dialogue comes from a bakery and mill near Berlin in Germany. Since 2009, *Märkisches Landbrot* has invited farmers in the region to join an annual roundtable dialogue. During the dialogue they discuss and agree on a price for grain for the year that works for all parties involved and creates stability and a clear planning horizon.[12]

Four Levels of Conversation

Similarly, there are four levels of conversation (see Figure 5.2):

- *Downloading* describes the first mode of conversation, one where we repeat familiar patterns: "How are you?" "I am fine." We politely say what others want to hear or what we think we are supposed to say. It is a form of *conforming* and staying inside our comfort zone.
- *Debate* moves beyond the comfort zone of politeness: "How are you?" "Okay, but I really take issue with what you said yesterday. I couldn't disagree more." The quality of conversation and attention heightens instantly, and the speakers share their different views. While this level of conversation is a step up from downloading because it reveals different views, it often comes with a limitation. In complex situations that require change and compromise, people tend to defend their own views and entrench themselves in their established positions. The recent trend of hyperpolarization has amplified this type of conversation in many ways. Polarization cannot be addressed without raising the

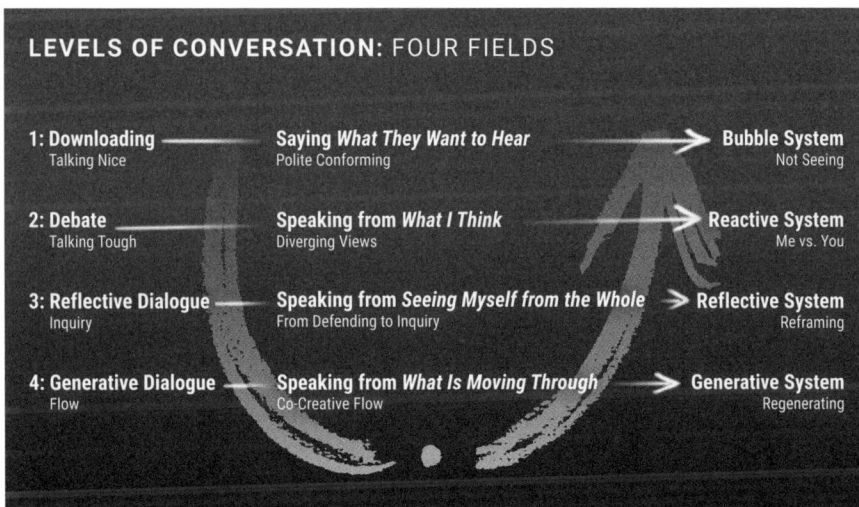

FIGURE 5.2: FOUR LEVELS OF CONVERSATION

conversational field to a new level and basically calls for conversation on Level 3 or 4.

- *Reflective dialogue* shifts the conversation into a different space. "Can you help me understand why you see it this way?" Rather than defensive routines, in a reflective dialogue we see inquiry. We see people with different views asking thoughtful questions of each other. Moving from debate to reflective dialogue requires a shift from rejecting the opposing view toward curiosity and inquiry. Reflective dialogue does not imply that everyone agrees; it is a shared process of reflection, perspective-taking, and inquiry. This form of dialogue leads to new insights and ideas.

- *Generative dialogue* deepens the conversation further. Picture a group of individuals sitting together in complete stillness, being deeply present with each other. When we stay in that deep and open space, the boundaries between us tend to shrink and new spaces of presence and possibility begin to open up. Something subtly new (or a subtle quality of presence) begins to show up. We are in a flow state of thinking, sensing, and creating together. The members of the group feel as if they can complete each other's sentences. Their sense of time slows down. The space is held open by generative listening, which is often called the invisible side of generative dialogue. Participants leave the space different—in a different or elevated state of awareness—than when they entered it.

These moments of deep connection are the backbone on which we can build new trust, new collaboration, and new eco-systemic societies and flourishing—which is something that in the years to come we will need just about *everywhere*.

Dialogue invites diverging views by *making space* and appreciating them. Dialogue is not just what happens when people talk to each other. Dialogue is the capacity of a system *to sense and see itself*, to bend the beam of observation back onto oneself. In a world where hyperpolarization, silencing, and othering keep us ever more separated and stuck, dialogue is the antidote.

Our colleague Julie Arts, who has led many profound change processes, shared her experience of creating a generative dialogue in her work with a research institute focused on the topic of rice in the Philippines, near Manila:

We were a very diverse group of young leaders, and we were about to visit rice farmers in the region. This group had done field trips before, but I decided to bring in the dialogue tool, generative dialogue being the fourth level. The group had many factual questions about farming: how they irrigate, what seeds they plant, how they're planted, how far the plants are apart, and then we suggest[ed] ways to have more yield especially given the climate change challenges. . . .

But I asked them to think of a generative question. And then one group came up with "Would you want your children to be rice farmers?" And for me, that's a brilliant question. If the answer is no, then there are deeper issues that we need to understand. So, we went to the fields, where I asked participants to witness and engage, not to just observe. Sit down with the farmers, listen to them. You're not trying to have an opinion, but you are just trying to be part of their lives for an hour. And then we set up small-group conversations with farmers, sometimes in the fields and sometimes in their gardens, or in front of their houses.

Then we all came back together, we ate something, and then did a reflection. Well, most farmers said no, they did not want their kids to be rice farmers. And the group realized that just to come in and suggest new irrigation techniques and better seeds will not be helpful. The most important learning had to do with the community pump. While not all children can go to school, one kid succeeded and became a politician. In that role he had organized a water pump for the community. That water pump had become a symbol of hope, and the researchers realized that their suggestions about new irrigation systems [had] included getting rid of that pump. So, if you come in and say, "This pump sucks. Your irrigation is done badly. We need to find another solution," you just rip the hope for their children apart. This conversation enabled participants to see and sense from the whole, and then co-create with the community instead of going in only with the intellect.[13]

Today, most leaders and many changemakers are unable to use the practice of generative dialogue. It is a largely missing skill. Conversational leadership is about *turning the collective attention around*, just as a farmer tills the soil or (in no-tilling agriculture) opens the surface of the soil. Methods include asking questions like, "Are we operating on the right level of conversation?" And if not, "How might we shift it?"

Dialogue is useful wherever people come together in circumstances where they hold *different* assumptions, worldviews, or material interests. One important approach is trauma-informed conflict resolution. The greater the diversity and depth of beliefs and experiences that people bring, the more important it is to move beyond polite downloading or traditional debate to the deeper levels of generative dialogue. Bill Isaacs, who has written about and worked with dialogue extensively, has referred to dialogue as *thinking together*.[14] Across sectors and systems we deal with situations that are dominated by reflexes, habits of *othering*, and *cancel cultures*—in short, situations where the spirit of dialogue is absent.

In the example that Julie shared, the dialogues with the rice farmers allowed everyone to sense a larger picture than technical and intellectual analysis of the situation would have allowed for. We call this *co-sensing*. Co-sensing is the capacity to sense a situation together from multiple perspectives simultaneously. It is the foundation for making systems see and sense themselves and thus is a foundational component of dialogue.

Creating and *holding spaces* for generative dialogue in complex high-stakes situations is one of the most critical leadership capacities for the future.

Tool: Building Containers

Each level of conversation has a role, function, and purpose. We need routine exchanges and open debates. But for real transformation we also need more complex conversations that involve reflective and generative dialogue. Leading transformation requires the ability to shift a conversation from one level to another and create the conditions for generative dialogue. How? The short answer is, by *building a container* that *holds space* for the dialogue.[15] The quality of a conversation is shaped by the quality of the container—the holding space that allows a conversation to shift to the next level.[16] Think of the container as the social soil: the quality of a conversation is a function of the quality of the social soil—the holding space from which a conversation emerges.

Our South African colleague Marian Goodman has conducted many complex and often difficult dialogues in her work. Her distinction between the inner and outer conditions of a container is important:

> Container building is a choreography of the inner and outer. The inner relates to your facilitation, not getting triggered by things that show up, holding the space of equanimity and attention with ease. I think inner ease is underrated. [The idea is] not to allow your own judgment or cynicism to even get a shoe in the door. Stay with whatever is happening without shutting it down, without fear, but listening for what's going to come up next. The outer comprises multiple aspects including the place or space, the timing, [and] the flow.[17]

Here are the first three core ingredients that build the inner conditions of a conversational container. By attending to them you can navigate the level of conversation as needed:

Shared intention: The more diverse the opinions and perspectives in a group, the more difficult but also more important it is to create a container. Aim to clarify the shared intention for the conversation so that it can be co-held by everyone involved. If it is difficult to clarify the intention with everyone involved, identify a core group member who can articulate the intention and then co-facilitate the conversation with you.

Focused and spacious time: Deepening a conversation does not happen by just adding another agenda item to an already long list, or by proclaiming, "Now, let's do dialogue." You can't expect everyone to just flip the switch and move from downloading or debate to a Level 3 or 4 conversation. Conversations are like *living fields* or a complex art installation. You need to set the intention, focus, and *tone* at the outset. A dialogue requires clarity of focus, as well as spaciousness that lets all the perspectives around the table be shared and heard.

A shared body of experience for co-sensing: In many projects we include opportunities for team members to go on learning journeys or field visits together. Our colleague Vanesa Weyrauch, who works in the field of policy and research in Latin America, often begins new projects with a slideshow of images; she invites everyone to pick one that reflects how they feel about the new project. She explains, "This exercise allows participants to hear from each other and creates a sense of the diverse views and perceptions around a shared beginning."[18] We describe this as co-sensing.

Below are some examples of how the first three steps were followed by groups we have encountered.

In one case, the leader of a complex, technology-related manufacturing firm placed a big piece of hardware in the center of the table and asked each participant to reflect and comment on the challenges related to that piece of hardware in their personal areas of responsibility. This exercise required everyone around the table, who worked in different functional areas of the company, to listen to each other. By the end of the meeting they had several concrete ideas about what to do next, and more important, they had a mutual understanding of how to proceed more efficiently.

In Nova Scotia we learned about the power of data-driven shared context creation from a non-profit organization called Engage Nova Scotia,[19] which surveyed local residents in the hope of developing a hyperlocal quality-of-life index. Danny Graham, their CEO, shared that the initiative was sparked by a desire to better support and understand the well-being of Nova Scotians and what they valued. When Engage asked Nova Scotia residents how they thought success should be measured, 58 percent said, "By growing the economy," but 82 percent said, "By improving our quality of life." Based on this response, Engage determined that "If we treasure it, we should measure it." So they embarked, in partnership with the Canadian Index of Wellbeing and groups across the province, in releasing the *Nova Scotia Quality of Life Index* in 2018 and the *Nova Scotia Quality of Life Survey* in 2019. The survey was the largest of its kind in North America, with 13,000 Nova Scotians responding to 230 questions each, what Danny describes "a mile deep and a mile wide."[20]

The hyperlocal data was captured on a platform where citizens and policy-makers could view the quality of life in their locality across many categories of citizens, such as young adults, seniors, single parents, people living with disabilities. In sensemaking workshops, local politicians and public decision-makers were guided through the data to both broaden and deepen their aware-ness of their communities' perceived well-being and collaborate to develop a vision for improvements. In a workshop held by Engage in one municipality, the lived experiences and challenges faced by different groups of Nova Scotians moved the policymakers toward shifting the strategic plan for their municipal-ity toward emphasizing social inclusion. Mayor Amanda McDougall notes, "What a long way we've come to making social inclusion a major part of our plan going forward. It really shows the impact of having the depth and breadth of data that Engage is able to provide. . . . It feels like we are heading in a direc-tion where no one will be left behind when making municipal decisions."[21]

Facilitation/leadership that embodies Level 4 principles: Participants in our workshops often remark on the quality of collaboration in our facilita-tion teams. The intention and quality of attention people embody as co-conveners matters. As our colleague Peter Senge likes to say: "The quality of relationships among the facilitators is the most powerful mech-anism for shifting the quality of the social field." Your interior condi-tion is part of the social field, and your quality of attention and spirit of genuineness directly influence the collective field of conversation. This applies whether you facilitate or participate in the conversation.

A shared body of collective deep listening: Cultivating the collective qual-ity of listening is essential for the success of a dialogue. While a dialogue might start with a group of individuals, the process of deep listening cul-tivates a *collective interior* space where what people were holding alone eventually is *co-held* by the whole circle or community. This process of personal sharing and collective deep listening provides strength and co-herence for the social field, for the group, for the organization, or for the community. Moments of deep collective listening are often critical in cultivating the social soil for subsequent evolutionary shifts.

Intentional stillness: Marian Goodman, who has facilitated numerous transformational interventions, shared an important learning about stillness: "I can only speak very personally here. Particularly when things get intense, I find myself going into an inner calm, deeper breathing. I know this also from my wilderness emergency training— you need to intentionally go still before you act."[22] When a workshop or team becomes "stuck," the next steps aren't always obvious. Instead of reacting quickly, here are two other good options to consider. One is to ask the people in the room what they think should be done. Usually, the group has a good answer. "When in doubt, always ask the client," our mentor at MIT Ed Schein used to say. Another option is *do nothing* but stay fully engaged with the situation. You don't intervene, you don't offer a solution or even different options. You do nothing. But you are fully present. A moment of stillness can allow the situation to clarify itself. Moments of stillness are not embarrassing gaps that need to be filled quickly; if they are held with presence, they can serve as a *gateway* to a deeper level of conversation. Sometimes intentional stillness occurs organically, while at other times it happens through a deliberate intervention such as a moment of mindfulness. Recall that the Eileen Fisher company begins its meetings with such a moment.

Aesthetic resonance: Resonance is an interesting word. Resonance is neither entirely objective (because it is experienced by the subject), nor is it entirely subjective (because it surfaces an *echo* of something that is experienced or seen). In other words, resonance is neither entirely *above* nor entirely *below* the ground of the social field. The word *aesthetics* comes from the Greek *aisthēsis*, which means perceiving with all your senses. It is, as our colleague and co-founder of the Presencing Institute Arawana Hayashi likes to say, the direct opposite of anesthesia. In other words, it's about *awakening* rather than numbing all of our senses.

Aesthetic resonance is a process that we first co-developed with our colleague Kelvy Bird. In its first iteration it was applied to *generative scribing,* a new social art that Kelvy developed and has written about.[23] Generative scribing is an evolved form of scribing that happens in real time during a workshop; it captures the essence of what happens above the ground (the content, what people say), as well as what happens below the ground in the social soil (what was felt and thought, as well as shifts in relationships and in consciousness).

At key junctures during a workshop, we gather the images and words that Kelvy (or another scribe) has captured in her drawings. In a moment of extended stillness, we take it all in. Instead of conducting an intellectualized interpretation or analysis, we fully attend to the deeper layers of resonance the images evoke among and within us. Then we ask participants to share their own resonance in a few words, using the following sentence structures:

"I see . . ."
"I sense . . ."
"I feel called to . . ."

Within minutes, that process of sharing creates a *deep scan* of the collective social field in the room. It also leads to a genuine experience of *seeing together*, of co-sensing, that deepens the level of connection among everyone in the room. In other words, it not only makes the social soil visible but also cultivates that soil by making the system see and sense itself.

We use this process a lot. Why? Even in large groups, the entire sequence described above usually takes no longer than ten minutes. And since all projects, processes, and multistakeholder initiatives are always short on time, that's a big plus.

This list of ingredients for building a conversational container is not exhaustive, but they are a good starting point. Yet social processes are not automatic or always predictable. Throwing ingredients into a bowl and mixing them up is not enough. A social process is an art more than a science. It requires constant awareness, full presence, and moment-to-moment adaptations. And it keeps emerging from the now.

Practice 4: Presencing: Meeting the Future that Stays in Need of Us in the Now

In the early days of the Covid-19 pandemic Otto returned to Boston on one of the last planes from Europe before the lockdown.

On that flight I began writing a blog about the current moment. Back in Boston, I had a call with some of the team in which we tried to make sense of it all. What's happening around us? What are we called to do now? Later that same day, I spoke to Antoinette Klatzky, a close friend, colleague, and fellow traveler who works in New York as a VP for the Eileen Fisher Foundation. I remember her saying, "What if now is the time?"

That question struck a chord. While my mind was still occupied with all the other plans that we had previously made for the following weeks, I could feel from the resonance in Antoinette's "what if" that something else was starting to open up and look at us—something that needed our attention. It was just a vague feeling that, whatever it was, it would likely move everything else into the background. Everything that wasn't essential would have to go.

In hindsight, we all know what happened. The world came to a stop. But at first, it wasn't obvious what would happen. Antoinette and I started to imagine what—if we pulled out all the stops—we could *do* at that moment. And suddenly we found ourselves in a flow. At the end of that conversation, we had mapped out an idea and intention that, deep in our hearts, we knew could be highly relevant to whatever was unfolding.

After that initial inspiration, I concluded my blog by suggesting a version of that idea: Let's all gather as a community online in the following week and co-sense into the current moment. What is happening around, between, and within us? How might we reimagine and reshape our journey forward, both individually and collectively?

GAIA: Global Activation of Intention and Action

The result was an initiative that we called GAIA (Global Activation of Intention and Action).[24] We envisioned it as a journey in which participants could, in the midst of what seemed like a moment of massive disruption, begin to identify their own inspirations, ideas, and initiatives for the future. GAIA would provide a collective space where people could experience a global field of resonance during this time of isolation, as well as have opportunities to connect locally.

We shared this idea with our community, our colleagues, and our friends. Within days, we enlisted the help of an amazing core team of about fifty volunteers, which later grew to two hundred. Over the next three months, we began hosting online conversations and co-facilitated biweekly activities involving a global community that grew to sixteen thousand participants. Some were colleagues and people we knew from earlier projects in various parts of the world; some were new people who simply showed up. We enlisted a technical partner that allowed us to host conversations among thousands of participants via Zoom and move between small groups and a large plenary. Small breakout groups were hosted by volunteers in more than eight languages, some with simultaneous translation. For the plenaries we hosted thought leaders, innovators, and changemakers from around the world who shared their how they made sense of the moment, their inspirations, and their ideas.

Each session incorporated practices of intentional stillness. Dropping into these moments of contemplation and presencing, not alone but in the context of a community of thousands, was a powerful experience. We heard some variation on these comments over and over again: "Being part of these moments of global stillness allowed me to connect to a deeper part of myself." "I thought I was alone and yet I've been able to connect with others who are thinking and feeling in the same ways I am, all over the world."

Antoinette remembers:

GAIA was a ray of sunshine in a dark time. When thousands of people around the world were dying alone and being carted off from hospitals by the truckload, we took a deep pause. In presencing, there is a space that opens up. The past is no longer there, and the future is not there yet. GAIA offered us a place to meet in that middle. Together, at the bottom of the U, at that moment of presence, we listened to each other, we listened to ourselves, we listened to the not-knowing and we listened to the deeper knowing.

When we slowed down that much, we were able to see the shadow of our societies, and once we saw these things, we couldn't unsee it. GAIA gave us an opportunity to see and sense together in order to take action in ways we likely never would have come up with before.[25]

Laura Pastorini, one of the key co-organizers of GAIA from South America, describes GAIA like this: "In a nutshell, GAIA became a global infrastructure for individuals and groups to meet, exchange, and get support throughout the Covid-19 pandemic in an innovative participatory online platform."[26] Many local and regional groups continued to collaborate after the pandemic. They produced countless new initiatives, one of which is the Ecosystem Leadership Program that we described in the previous chapter, which links and co-inspires hundreds of changemakers across Latin America.

One example of how GAIA's collective space allowed local groups to connect and begin to address their challenges is the project Querétaro es Uno in Mexico, led by Willy Azarcoya and his team.[27] In one GAIA session a participant from Switzerland had expressed the idea that we need more "micro solidarity." That idea resonated with the team in Mexico. Willy recalls:

> We said, that's it. We should work in micro solidarity, and let's see what emerges from this. We began to build a small prototype with three objectives: to help the most vulnerable people, help the medical sector, and explore the concept of a circular economy. . . . Four weeks after that we had forty organizations, from NGOs to concerned citizens. . . . We built a website, and after eight weeks we had distributed 400 pounds of food. And the medical supplies appeared from nowhere. I can't explain it. It was just like [a] magical eco-system that was invisible before and became suddenly visible. For example, restaurants said, "We are closed, but you can use our kitchens." Or hospitals said, "We can be a place where people can bring stuff." . . . There were a lot of little efforts working all around. It was trust, pure trust.[28]

This initiative ended up donating medical supplies and over 600 tons of food.[29]

Today this initiative has become Learning City Leadership Lab. UNESCO has declared Querétaro a "learning city" based on the results of this initiative. In many parts of the world, we have met people who years later tell us what a profound difference GAIA made in their lives and in their capacity to redirect their personal and professional journeys.

Reflecting back to the beginning moments, it always felt that the idea of launching GAIA did not emerge from thin air. Antoinette and I felt as if something might be possible, something that could be activated. The moment you feel the presence of that possibility, it is almost impossible to *not do it*. All it required was to stop. It required our full attention to an idea that was already there. It just needed us to provide a *landing space*. When everyone else showed up, it felt as if our *individual and collective boundaries collapsed* or, to use another word, *opened*.

When people share what the GAIA experience meant to them, we often hear thoughts like these:

"It saved me in a very challenging moment when I truly needed help. It gave me hope."

"It helped me to reimagine, and then reshape, my life and work—I changed my entire career and I am living it now."

"It connected me with a group of people that I didn't know before and some of which I am still in very close contact with. With some of them I even co-founded a new organization. They are my partners now."

GAIA is an example of how, in very difficult times, we can collectively step into a future potential and *activate agency* at a massive scale. This is essentially what the practice of presencing is about.

To Align Attention, Intention, and Agency

Presencing is the practice of meeting the future that is in need of us in the now. It is the most critical capacity of eco-system leadership. Presencing is both personal and collective. It is the source for aligning attention, intention, and agency by deepening our connection to what arises from the now.

What is the difference between attention and intention? The difference is in the *relationship* between the mind and the world. When using the word *attention*, we mean a stretching or focusing of the mind toward something, some kind of object, that usually belongs to a world that exists *separately* from the observer. The object is there. I (the observer) am here. I am stretching my attention toward the object, focusing on it. In that sense it is about taking notice, taking in.

In contrast, the word *intention* is not based on separation but on *oneness*. My mind is oriented toward a seed or a future potential that hasn't fully materialized. My intention extends to a reality that is not separate or outside of me but deeply connected to me; it may be in the process of manifesting *through me*. My mind is oriented toward something that is emerging from or through our inner sources of knowing, holding the space for something that isn't quite there yet.

Attention focuses the mind on something outside of us, whereas *intention* orients us toward a purpose in a less visible realm, which could be thought of as source dimension of a reality that has not fully manifested as of yet. Attention is an activity of the mind, and intention is also an activity of the heart and hand.

The difference can be further clarified by the distinction between intention and goal, two terms that are often confused. A *goal* is something *out there*. It's a clear set of outcomes. For example, in the context of a hike, the goal might be reaching the mountaintop. But an *intention* is deeper and includes the interior condition. It orients you to the goal but is *present with you during the entire hike* to the top. It is embodied every step of the way and guides you throughout the journey. A goal is something that you connect to with your head. An intention is something you can only connect with through your whole being—your head, heart, and hands.

The Essence of Theory U

The essence of eco-system leadership is about aligning attention, intention, and agency. This alignment of a social field requires a process. We call this the *U-process* or *Theory U*.[30] Color Plate 1 outlines the three core components of the process:

> **going down the left side of U**: sense from the edges of the system with your mind and heart wide open
> **bottom of the U**: being present; allowing inner knowing to emerge

going up the right side of the U: envision, embody, and explore the future
by doing

Today we would summarize the same core process with just three words:
attention, intention, and agency (see Color Plate 2).

When our attention and intention are aligned, we call it *mindfulness*. It's a
critical tool for focusing on our way down the left side of the U (Color Plates
1 and 2). All contemplative practices require the alignment of attention and
intention in one way or another.

When we align our attention with action (but without intention), we call
this a *reactive response*: going straight from a perceived problem (attention) to
a solution (action). On the positive side, this can happen quickly. On the negative side, it may keep us stuck in past patterns.

When we align intention and agency (without attention), we call it *mindless
action*: implementing without learning. We move from an idea to implementation without attending to, learning from, and adjusting to the relevant contexts.

The integration of all three—attention, intention, and agency—is what we
call *presencing-based leadership*. It is a core process that goes through two major
turns:

attention: if broadened and deepened, gives rise to intention.
intention: if deepened and clarified, catalyzes agency.

At the heart of those two turns—which happen at the bottom of the U—is
presencing: the capacity to be fully present to what is and what is emerging
from meeting the moment. That is what happened when Antoinette asked
"What if now is the time?" That's also what happened in the multistakeholder
process that Manish described. When the attention of the group shifted and
participants were able to stop and listen to the perspectives of the women in
the room, attention was inverted and the collective intention to fight child hun-
ger emerged, and ultimately led to the activation of profound agency.

We grow in the direction of the attention and intention that we embody and
focus on. When you place your attention on your *intention*, you begin to water

the seeds. When your attention is overly focused on what you don't want—on what you want to avoid—you are at risk of watering the wrong seeds. This is why hyperpolarization tends to lead to collective paralysis.

Agency will ultimately die if you don't make yourself an instrument of a deeper intention that you hold in your life. When you do that, the first thing that tends to happen is: nothing. Nothing happens. Then you keep going, placing your attention on your deepest intention and making your Self an instrument of it. Then that intention slowly begins to activate a field that attracts helping hands and agency. That process can take quite a while—years or more than a decade—or, as in the case of GAIA, it can happen in days.

As visualized in Inserts 1 and 2, on the journey down the left side of the U, *the beam of attention* bends back to the "source" through the gestures of *suspending, redirecting,* and *letting go.* Presencing is the source practice at the bottom of the U. It's a dormant human capacity that in principle can be activated anytime, anywhere. Presencing is the moment that opens our attention in ways that give rise to our emerging intention. In Manish's story, it was the moment in the dialogue when the commitment in the group emerged.

Cognitively, the journey down the U can be seen as an *inversion* of attention: the object or phenomenon that you are attending to from different angles (like child nutrition) becomes a holding space, which then gives rise to something new (deep intention).

The journey up the right side of the U is about holding the space for something to clarify, crystallize, grow, and evolve. Throughout this part of the journey, you are passing through the same gates or gestures (*suspending, redirecting* from object to source, *letting go*), but in the other direction: *letting come, redirecting* from source to prototype, and *enacting.* Going up the righthand side of the U involves allowing the deeper intention to manifest.

The framework of Theory U is based on four levels of awareness and consciousness that give rise to different qualities of relationships. These types of consciousness and relationships are reflected in the distinction between the four hemispheres of the Wheel of Deep Change (see Foldout Color Plate 1).

Observations on Leading Presencing Processes

In real-world applications in teams, organizations, and larger systems, the U process is made practical through a core process of five movements (see Color Plate 3):

Co-initiating: Share context and uncover common intent.

Co-sensing: Go to the edges of the system and listen with your mind and heart wide open.

Co-presencing: Go to a place of stillness and allow your inner knowing to emerge.

Co-creating: Explore the future by doing—by prototyping and iterating.

Co-evolving: Embody the new in practices and supporting infrastructures.

Since the publication of the Theory U framework, we and many others have taken groups through this kind of transformation journey on countless occasions. Although the five movements are universal, any intervention is context specific.

Having undertaken this process over the years with many thousands of people, we have seen certain similarities that cut across systems, sectors, and cultures. Here are some observations in regard to presencing:

- There is a profound quieting, slowing down, and entry into a space of stillness (suspension).

- Stillness is the state that lets a deeper layer of awareness open up. You begin to see or sense yourself from a different vantage point (attention is redirected).

- You recognize patterns of behavior that are often shaped by habits and/ or exterior forces. Your attention begins to happen from a higher vantage point (sensing).

- As you surrender to what's essential, and as you let go of *everything that isn't*, a different and much shorter list of true (purpose-related) priorities becomes clear (letting go, letting come).

- The quality of the group container—which holds the shared social soil—is critical for entering, deepening, and sustaining this sense of deep presence.
- Solo in nature, social art practices, and presencing practices serve as reliable gateways into the deeper realms of the experience.
- Human relationships that are developed in this context can activate profound connections across stark differences in ideology, identity, worldview, and culture. Diverse groups can activate *generative social fields* that create love, friendship, support, and a constant stream of new inspirations, initiatives, and ideas.

Tool: Learning How to Stop

In retreat workshops we give participants practices that help them to slow down and look at themselves from a higher vantage point. Often, they come to realize how much of their everyday behavior is conditioned by their environment and that there is a whole other landscape of being, connecting, living, and working. But listening deeply to each other's unfolding journey is where a lot of the group magic originates. In holding space for such a process, intentional stillness tends to be one of the most important gateways.

Here are some core principles:

Stop: slow down to stillness.
Let go: let go of focused attention and allow open awareness to emerge.
Be present: after stopping and letting go, do nothing, but remain fully present.
Go with the flow: if something begins to emerge, be present with it and stay with it.

There are many ways to design the moment of stopping and let go. Solo experiences in nature accompanied by reflective practices can be very powerful. The IDEAS Indonesia journey includes a four-day presencing retreat that always begins with co-sensing practices, deepens with presencing practices, and concludes with the formation of cross-sector prototyping teams. At the heart of the retreat workshop is a journaling and visioning practice, followed

by a half-day solo retreat in nature. We conclude the retreat by forming a circle in which everyone shares some part of their experience. The experiences
shared in these circles are always connected to the edge of one's not-knowing,
discomfort, and essence. Frequently, participants describe the circle reflections
as a turning point or as like being "born for a second time," meaning connecting to their life's purpose much more deeply and clearly.

   This is what presencing is primarily about: connecting with and operating
from one's highest future possibility, a deepened sense of what we are here for.

   For more detail and other tools and resources, visit u-school.org.

Practice 5: Co-imagining—Holding Space for Crystallizing the Future That We Want to Create

While all systems thinking involves attending to the whole, traditional forms
of systems thinking can be quite analytical and focused on the upper half of
the Wheel. This is why, as indicated in Foldout Color Plate 1, systems thinking can evolve into or be complemented by systems sensing—moving our
cognition from the head to the heart—and with systems awareness or presencing, by which we mean an evolved systems thinking and systems sensing
that operates from the future wanting to emerge. At this point in the process, as
we are beginning to emerge from the bottom of the U, there are three interre-
lated things going on:

   Landing the intention: A true deep intention is not your own brainchild. It
      is the highest future potential *looking at* you. It can be vague or clear,
      but generally it tends to be amorphous and unspecified. "Landing" the
      intention means clarifying that intention. What is it? Can you listen to
      it? In Theory U we refer to this as "crystallizing" your intention.

   Unconditional commitment: This is where the magic comes in. Uncondi-
      tional commitment is not rational. If it were, it would be conditional.
      Unconditional commitment means: YES—I am ALL IN. It's what my
      father said when he encountered a new idea in agriculture. It's the most
      sacred yes that we as humans can offer to the universe. You may have

no idea what it is that you are saying yes to. It is a moment Goethe describes like this:

> Concerning all acts of initiative (and creation), there is one elementary truth, the ignorance of which kills countless ideas and splendid plans: that the moment one definitely commits oneself, then Providence moves too. All sorts of things occur to help one that would never otherwise have occurred. . . . *Whatever you can do or dream you can, begin it. Boldness has genius, power, and magic in it!*[31]

Co-imagining the future that you want to create: This imagining entails creating living images of the future that you want to manifest.

The first element—letting the intention talk to you, letting it land—is about humble listening. It's the antidote to ego, arrogance, and hubris. The second element—unconditional commitment—is about the sacred yes. It's the antidote to the prevailing paralysis. The third element—co-imagining the future that you want to create—is about realigning attention and intention at the scale of the whole. It's the antidote to today's dominant dystopian views of the future.

These elements, if nurtured together, form a seed of the future. A seed is barely visible but holds the full future potential that we want to create. That seed of the future can feel like an alien element. "Alien" means here that it has its own intentionality and perhaps even its own voice, if only we can be receptive enough to truly listen to it. That seed is something that we can be in *inner dialogue* with, as many of the greatest authors, creators, innovators, and founders constantly *are*.

The Power of Intention

Here we recount two recent examples in which we experienced this moment of intention that we could not ignore.

u-lab

In 2013 we sat with Dayna Cunningham, co-founder and then executive director of the MIT Community Innovators Lab, and Phil Thompson, Urban Studies professor and later deputy mayor of New York, in a conference room.

Phil had just shared his take on a faculty meeting in which then MIT President Rafael Reif had announced the reinvention of learning at MIT. We (Otto and Katrin) looked at each other and realized that this was exactly what we were doing with the Presencing Institute.

But then, we also felt a sense of frustration. No one had asked us to join the conversation. Nevertheless, the subsequent discussion among the four of us prompted me (Otto) to write an email to the MIT president the next morning, to which he replied within a few hours. He directed me to meet with the vice president of MIT Open Learning, Sanjay Sarma. When we met, Sanjay shared his vision for Open Learning at MIT and suggested that I take the u-lab class that I was teaching at the MIT Sloan School of Management to the MITx platform, to allow for worldwide free access. We did that. And that was how the u-lab on MITx with 260,000 registered users was born. In summary, we did the following:

- landed the intention, in this case through the gateway of frustration;
- received unconditional commitment (this happened when I responded to Sanjay's invitation with a yes and teamed up with our colleague Adam Yukelson to make it happen); and
- co-imagined the future (this happened when Adam, together with me and few others, envisioned the entire platform and all its novel features in an amazingly co-creative period of our lives).

Ecosystem Leadership Program Latin America (ELP LATAM)

The landing of the idea for ELP Latin America happened when Laura and Otto sat together after the one-day workshop in Santiago, Chile.

We were talking about how well it had gone. Laura said, "Look, *this* is what we need all over the place. And it's needed now." That was the moment when we not only felt that the regional intention was looking *at us* (or landing); we also felt it synching with our own intention and commitment to make it happen *no matter what* (unconditional commitment). That commitment was later replicated and strengthened by the team that Laura co-convened (co-imagining the future).

Tool: Identifying the Seeds of the Future

In conclusion, there are three elements that, if cultivated together, help us to connect to our deeper sources of intention and creativity. For these seeds of the future to take root, they need quality soil. How do we provide that soil? As the stories in this chapter make clear, even small core groups of two to three people can create the fertile ground that the seeds need to sprout and thrive. In other words, any of us can do it.

Eco-system leadership requires creating the right soil conditions. These conditions are highly contextual. They differ depending on whether the seed is intended for personal, organizational, or societal regeneration and transformation.

One tool that we developed at the Presencing Institute is a template for framing a discussion about what the seed needs in order to grow: For your initiative to succeed, what soil, water, air, and light do you need?[32] When we ask these questions, sometimes the answer is "a protected space for small experiments." Peter Senge, our colleague at MIT, sometimes jokes that you don't pull the carrot out of the ground again and again to check how it is growing. The same applies to change initiatives.

Arawana Hayashi, co-founder of the Presencing Institute and creator of the social art form social presencing theater, has developed the Seed Dance, which invites participants to lean into the intention they hold and find ways to express the first small step with a gesture and then a word or a sentence. It is an embodied learning practice that we have found to be very helpful.[33]

Practice 6: Co-creating—Holding Space for Exploring the Future by Doing

The practice of co-creation is about exploring the future through experimentation and doing. The secret of successful prototyping is to translate big and bold ideas into something small and doable that creates useful feedback for further refining the idea. One way to test the quality of a prototyping idea is to ask these seven questions:

- Is it relevant? Does it really matter to the key stakeholders?
- Is it new or revolutionary? Could it change the game?
- Is it regenerative? Does it move beyond extraction?
- Can it be done quickly on a small scale?
- Can you see the whole in the microcosm you are focusing on?
- Is it relationally effective? Does it leverage the people in the room/in your network?
- Is it replicable? Can you bring it to meaningful scale?

Holding these co-creative spaces requires attention, intention, and tools. There are many techniques of co-creation, depending on the context and people involved. Designing and holding such spaces requires presence and learning from context. It's a form of embodied learning through direct interaction with stakeholders, through deep listening and generative dialogue. Here is one example from Indonesia.

From Illegal Logging and Deforestation to Sustainable Timber Economies

Some of the largest rainforests in the world are located in Indonesia. Almost 75 percent of the 120 million hectares of Indonesian forest are in critical condition due to illegal logging. Indonesia's rapid deforestation has dire implications for economic, human, and planetary health. Yet the country is also emerging as a bright spot in the fight against illegal logging. According to the World Resources Institute, in 2020, Indonesia ranked first in deforestation reduction for the fourth year in a row.[34]

One of the IDEAS fellows in Indonesia, Silverius Oscar Unggul, better known as Onte, has worked passionately to stop illegal logging across Indonesia for the past three decades. While a university student, Onte and his friends began by establishing their own radio station, Suara Alam (Voice of Nature), to broadcast local stories about illegal logging and environmental destruction, and later they ventured into television to amplify their message and raise community engagement. Their efforts eventually contributed to large-scale advocacy campaigns, which gained international attention and finally led the Indonesian government to crack down on illegal logging.

However, Onte and his team soon noticed a trend: while the larger extractive industry remained, only the "small" players were being arrested—some of them were local villagers whom Onte had come to know personally. This marked a turning point for him, as he felt they had failed in his mission. "Only the small people were being sent to jail," he recalls. Then a new idea emerged: Why not collaborate with the illegal loggers instead, and help them transition into sustainable logging practices that would also shift economies away from extractive industry? To do that, he would first spend weeks living in the forests, moving from place to place with the illegal loggers.[35]

Onte recounts: "It all started from a small village near Kendari, southeast Sulawesi. I watched my friend being arrested for logging without a legal permit. I realized that numerous [laws] passed on natural resources management had caused the loss of locals' harvesting rights in managing their long-accustomed resources."[36] As Onte lived with the loggers to better understand them and their situation, he shared meals with them around their camp and they spoke together about their lives and their families. As he tells it: "Every night we talked, and we asked, what are your dreams? I found that for us, it's very easy to say, 'I have a dream.' But for people who are suffering, it is difficult. The response was often 'Oh, no, no. We have no dream. We just wanted to make money to feed our family.'" One night, Onte asked a different question: "If something happened to you, you got sick, do you want your children to follow in your footsteps?" "No, I hope not," was the reply. "I don't want them in this business." This started a conversation about ways to make sustainable livelihoods that can sustain generations and protect the forest. "Our job is to inspire them to dream, to have a simple dream," Onte realized. "Developing the dream comes first, for without dreams, there's no motivation."[37]

From these conversations the idea of local cooperatives was born. Starting with a group of just seven families, today the cooperatives are comprised of thousands. These community-based logging cooperatives have made sustainable forestry a viable alternative for formerly illegal loggers across Indonesian provinces, using a sustainable forestry certification process and, as they have grown and multiplied, establishing cooperative networks.[38] Onte was later appointed to Indonesia's Chamber of Commerce as its chairperson for

Environment and Forestry. He was the first social entrepreneur to hold this position, and in it he could continue to support both community livelihoods and the preservation of the forests.

Principles of Co-Creation

The seed in Onte's story is his deep commitment to the forests of Indonesia—in fact, his involvement began with a group he founded as a college student dedicated to spending time in forests and mountains, where he also found community and hosts in the local villages surrounding the forests, as well as the deforestation brought about by illegal logging. The breakthrough in Onte's journey occurred when he stepped into the experience of the local illegal logger. This embodied experience became an opportunity for deep sensing and co-creation. Here are some core principles of co-creation:

Big things start small: Any change or transformation begins with a small island of coherence—sometimes with just one or two people.

Form an intentional core group: To make things happen, you need to team up. A core group or team that aligns around an intention is a powerful force. We sometimes suggest that the diversity of the core group should reflect the diversity of the stakeholders in the issue that you are trying to address (if possible).

Listen and dialogue with your mind and heart wide open—and dream forward: Onte and his friends generated their most important ideas while living with the affected communities in the forests. Their openness to listening to the reality on the ground is foundational for a co-creation process. Attention to and immersion in place are a gateway to sourcing ideas and solutions.

Explore your ideas by doing, listen to the feedback, and iterate: The first step toward a transformation is small, and it is followed by many iterations. These iterations are an important part of the process. Don't consider them failures but opportunities to learn.

Always cultivate the power of intention and place: Iterations require ongoing clarification as well as a dialogue with the evolving intention that sparked the initiative. We work with GLS Bank, a German bank that fo-cuses on social, cultural, and ecological initiatives. One of the bank's co-founders described the power of intention as follows: "You cannot overcome your angst of the future you fear without an image of the future that you want."[39]

Tool: Prototyping—A Tool for Embodied Learning

The creative process requires spaces as well as techniques. Co-creation is not about finding the one right answer or brilliant idea. Co-creation is an explora-tion, a journey that requires presence and an ongoing dialogue with the future that you want to be in service of and to co-create.

One technique that furthers the process of exploration is prototyping.[40] There are many approaches to prototyping, but here is a brief introduction.

A prototype is an exploration of the possible future through experimenta-tion. We often make the distinction between a prototype and a pilot. A proto-type is rapid and iterative and is intended to provide quick learning and feedback. A pilot is carefully planned and is designed to prove why a specific idea or solution works. One useful resource for prototyping is the Innova-tors' Compass launched by our colleague Ela Ben-Ur, which provides a great tool for prototyping.[41]

The purpose of prototyping is to "fail early to learn quickly." A process of trial and error takes the innovator through several iterations of an idea based on feedback from stakeholders. This feedback informs the refinement of the original concept or idea and its underlying assumptions. Lessons learned through prototyping are the basis for scaling up or institutionalizing an idea or practice.

There are two patterns that often get in the way of effective prototyping. One is known as analysis-paralysis. It's the tendency to discuss and analyze things to death. It involves questions, followed by more questions, which in reality are just resistance to moving into action in disguise. The remedy is: Yes, let's do it. Or: Sense it, feel it, do it.

Analysis-paralysis reflects an *actionless mind*. The second pattern is *mindless action*—that is, implementation without any sensing, adapting, and learning.

Prototyping is the art of the middle way, not getting lost in either of these two ways of disconnecting.

Practice 7: Eco-system Governance—Holding Space for Coordinating around Shared Intention

Eco-system governance is about organizing and coordinating around shared intention. Governance is the coordination of patterns of collaboration across people, teams, institutions, businesses, communities, nations, and eco-systems.

In working toward appropriate responses to the polycrisis at all levels (micro, meso, macro, and mundo), governance plays a key role. The gap between the 69 percent who are willing to make personal sacrifices to advance solutions that address our climate challenges and our actual collective decision-making falls massively short of this aspiration and illustrates in a nutshell the governance challenge we are up against.

What makes eco-systemic governance effective? Let's take the example of microfinance. In the 1980s microfinance was hyped and celebrated as a solution to poverty, but it quickly became clear that some microfinance organizations provided workable and constructive options, while others did not. The difference was in the intentions of the leadership and governance teams: one group primarily wanted to maximize profit, while the other combined profitability with transforming the lives of their customers.

Eco-system governance presents a coordination challenge that cannot be solved by simply adding another layer of structures and regulations to an already overregulated landscape. In fact, when we look at the mechanisms that the progressive movement has used to advance a more sustainable and equitable agenda in our society, what are we noticing? The overemphasis on Level 2 governance. The result is an ever-growing layer of bureaucratic regulations that increasingly limit the creative capacities of people on the frontline of delivery (teachers, doctors, farmers, entrepreneurs, etc.). So, yes, we do need innovation in regulation. But what we also need is the right intention. In an era marked by widespread deregulation across various regions, the need to upgrade and adapt our governance frameworks will become increasingly vital in shaping sustainable and equitable futures.

The evolution from 2.0 to 4.0 forms of coordination is a journey of interiorizing governance. It's a journey from exterior mechanisms of coordination that operate through external incentives (markets) or commands (hierarchies) to complementary interior mechanisms that are organized around shared intention and catalyze collective action.

National and Customary Forest Governance in Indonesia

Before he joined the IDEAS program, Bambang Supriyanto was head of the Halimun-Salak National Park, which manages conservation forests covering an area of 113,357 hectares located in two Indonesian provinces, West Java and Banten. Bambang sought to both ensure the preservation of biodiversity and habitat and ensure the existence and quality of life of 314 sub-villages and 11 customary or Indigenous (Adat) communities inside the national park. In Indonesia, the world's third most populous democracy spread over a vast territory of 17,000 islands, multiculturalism is central. There are 1,128 ethnic tribes and 718 languages spread across 76,655 villages in the archipelago.

Bambang was taking all he had learned from national park management to a position in the national Ministry of Forestry when a Supreme Court decision in 2012 ruled that "customary forests," where Indigenous communities often lived and practiced their traditional (customary) use of forests in their territories, should be returned to those communities' legal control. At the time of the ruling, all land in Indonesia designated as forest areas fell under the control of the state. It was a landmark decision for Indigenous communities; however, following it there was no progress. Several ministries objected to formally acknowledging the customary forest area, and as a result, the Supreme Court decision was not being implemented.

Bambang saw that acknowledgment of customary Indigenous forests would be crucial for both the eco-system and the communities living there, and that the customary communities would protect the forests with sustainable forest management practices. For customary forest acknowledgment to occur, certain criteria needed to be met, and this required coordination from multiple stakeholders. Bambang recognized that the implementation was stuck in place. He realized he would need to instill confidence in the Minister of Environment and Forestry that implementation could be successful and, as he recalls, to show that "what the stakeholders hoped for wasn't in contradiction."[42] This intention would lead Bambang and his team to develop processes and innovations to help communities navigate barriers and meet criteria, and to seed the social fields of the customary forest acknowledgment process across Indonesia.

Starting in Halimun-Salak National Park where he had worked for many years, and using the methods and tools that he learned as an IDEAS fellow, Bambang prototyped what would later become the integrated team process that navigated requirements, conflicts, and coordination. As part of his IDEAS prototype work, he began a learning journey that included park officers, forest rangers, heads of Indigenous communities, advisory heads of customary communities, heads of villages, and the voiceless stakeholders: the forests themselves and their wildlife. His interviews and dialogues with and among these stakeholders revealed a common vision of coexisting in harmony. Bambang crystallized this learning into a common purpose: a community-based National Park Management Plan. He also recognized the need for a joint mapping process by the national park and the Indigenous communities. As these aspects developed, Bambang facilitated detailed communication, which enabled all parties to meet and listen, discuss an agreement, and document it.

Bambang presented the results to the Minister of Environment and Forestry. It worked. "I had the opportunity to convince him that acknowledgment of customary law communities and their living space could be carried out immediately," Bambang said.[43]

The momentum for recognition of customary forests began to build after that. In 2017, Bambang was promoted to be director general of Social Forestry and Environmental Partnerships of Indonesia, which enabled him to accelerate and improve on the acknowledgment of customary law communities and their living spaces. Bambang was now the government official authorized to issue the Adat/Customary Forest Decrees. As of 2023, almost 6.5 million hectares of legal access have been granted for 9,719 villages and 138 customary forests have been acknowledged, covering an area of 265,250 hectares.

Learnings on Holding Space

Here are some of the main things learned from this case:

To heal our relationship with nature (and move from extractive to regenerative practices), we must also heal our relationships with each other: Moving from the structural violence of exclusion to inclusion, self-governance, and dignity required a multistakeholder process that included all parties involved. In hindsight, Bambang realizes that the multistakeholder process that emerged from the prototype in the Halimun-Salak park formed many of the connections and trust relationships that later allowed him to establish a more participative eco-system governance system. The process supported Adat (customary) people and simultaneously coordinated the activities of the ministries and stakeholders, instead of leaving each to operate in its own silo.

A key enabler of this outcome was co-sensing, a process of listening, dialogue, and building trust: In the co-sensing stage of the prototype, Bambang was the "first facilitator" for bringing the different stakeholder groups together, a role that is now institutionalized and professionalized across the agencies that support the implementation of customary forest management.

Listening is an ongoing key practice: Bambang's colleague, Yuli Prasetyo, emphasized in his reflection that focusing on listening is critical. "We join the people, research, participation process. We are working there; [it involves] not just paperwork or policy, but listening and more listening, especially about customary people."

Respect is our responsibility: Yuli Prasetyo added that "every stakeholder can respect the results because they are involved in the process. From the central government, to the local government, the civil society, the head of the village, and the heads of the customary communities, of course. So it is *our* responsibility, not *your* responsibility."[44]

Distributed governance is key: The solution allowed for a distributed eco-system governance between the national and the local levels leading to increased local agency.

Eco-system governance anchors the six other practices of eco-system leadership by creating processes and structures that are transparent, reliable, and adaptable. These structures and processes allow for whole-system learning that shares innovation from one place to others.

We began this chapter with Otto's father's life-altering lesson that the regeneration of our planet's soil requires the regeneration of community—what we call our social soil. We can add that, in order to make this work we need to transform our societal operating systems from 1.0 and 2.0 to 4.0, which in turn requires us to upgrade our leadership capacities, as exemplified by the stories above.

Chapter 6

The Future Is Already Here

Three Transformations

We opened this book by talking about the silent revolution that we see emerging in many places across the planet and around the world. It's a subtle inner shift of awareness that runs much deeper than any of the current political shifts or divides. It cuts across them and manifests as a widespread desire for regeneration, healing, and flourishing. We link that new awareness to the cultivation of the less visible half of the Wheel of Deep Systems Change, the *social soil*. Seven practices, if put to work, cultivate the social soil for the manifold transformations to come.

As we experience the fragility of our planet, of our societies, and also of our own selves we must keep in mind three important considerations:

- Anyone who is paying attention knows that we have entered uncharted territory. We are (a) massively overusing planetary resources, (b) escalating the risk of nuclear war, and (c) most of the time silently accepting inequalities and social divides.
- There is the astonishing self-healing capacity of the biosphere: the capacity of Mother Earth to revive and regenerate the moment we begin to

shift our collective behavior from extraction to regeneration and healing. Plus, the transformation of the human spirit does not happen one step at a time but can happen in an instant, all at once.

• All the solutions that we need to end the polycrisis are already available, whether it is in energy, food, poverty alleviation, health, learning, or governance, to mention a few. The future, or more precisely, the seeds of the future, are already here. But we're missing the soil that would allow these seeds to flourish.

That is the focus of this chapter.

The opening question of this book is: *Are we sinking, or are we going to rise?* The answer to the question is an existential one. The only place that it can be answered from is the *heart*. The *opening* or the *closing* of the heart accounts for the difference between activating the cycle of presencing and creation and activating the cycle of absencing and destruction. The opening of the heart requires cultivation practices and courage; it requires inner leadership work that aligns attention, intention, and agency and allows us to recognize the potential of the future that is already here. We take inspiration from the following lines:

> *We must root out from the depths of our soul the fear and dread of what the future may bring. . . . We must face whatever may come with absolute equanimity, trusting that whatever arrives is guided by the wisdom of the cosmos. In every moment, our task is to do what is right and leave everything else to the unfolding of time. In these days, we must learn to live out of pure trust. . . . Truly, there is no other way if we are to keep our courage from sinking. Let us strengthen our will and seek inner awakening, each morning and each evening.*[1]

Courage in the face of fear. Equanimity in the face of discomfort. Trust in the face of not-knowing. These are the virtues or access points of our deeper sources of knowing that, if cultivated, help us to move forward.

Seed Meditation: Earth Rise

Cultivating the leadership skills that allow us to align attention, intention, and agency takes practice. We invite you now to the following experimental seed meditation that will allow you to step out of the day-to-day into a broader perspective.

Imagine we can zoom out and look back at planet Earth from space. The farther we zoom out, the smaller the planet looks. When it looks as tiny as a grain of dust in the vast universe, it's hard to imagine it could have any significance.

But what if we look at that speck of dust as if it were a seed waiting to emerge from its seed coat? What if that tiny particle of dust holds the potential for something special and precious to manifest? Hold that possibility in your mind as you pay attention to our planet. Hold your gaze steady.

At the same time, remember that only one part of us is zoomed out and looking back from space—the observer within us. The other part of us is still connected to the living planet. It's not just that we are living *on* the planet. In many ways we also *are* the living planet. Our bodies are made of the same physical and biochemical components as the planet. We are, literally, earth dust. Our big body (planet Earth) and our small body (our physical body) are composed of roughly the same amount of water (60–70 percent). In most of humanity's wisdom traditions we find echoes of an ancient idea that humans are microcosms of the larger macrocosm. The word origin of humanity and earth (humus) is one and the same, suggesting that humans are "earthlings."

This microcosm–macrocosm relationship is also reflected in rhythms. For example, our planet not only rotates on its own axis once every 24 hours (creating the rhythm of day and night) but also around the sun (creating the cycle of seasons). It has a much longer cycle as well. Imagine our planet as a spinning top whose axis leans a little bit as it spins (by 23.5°, to be precise). As a result, sometimes one side of Earth gets more sun, making it warmer and brighter (summer), and sometimes it gets less sun, making it colder and darker (winter). Now, imagine this leaning planet keeps slowly rotating. Each rotation cycle takes a long time, roughly 26,000 years to finish just once—that cycle is called the Great Year. During an average lifetime of roughly seventy years, human beings live for about 26,000 days. This is the same number! In other words, in an average lifetime, humans live as many daily rotations on Earth as the Earth takes around the sun to complete one Great Year. Microcosm and macrocosm are woven into each other in manifold ways.

While in our awareness we continue to hold our attention on the small blue marble or grain of dust that is Earth, and the dormant qualities surrounding it, we now also expand our awareness to include *ourselves*. Our self relates to the planet just as the planet relates to the macro universe: as a seed or grain of dust inside yet another grain of dust (our blue planet). This is seemingly insignificant. But it means we are present in both places: we are the *Seer* who is becoming aware of all this "from outer space"; and we are also present *inside* the grain of dust that is the very subject of that awakening awareness.

With that unfolding situation in the back of our mind, let us now contemplate the account by one of the first people to actually experience seeing our planet from space, the astronaut Rusty Schweickart. In 1969, Rusty flew on the Apollo 9 mission that preceded the first moon landing. In a 1974 speech, he said it had taken him five years to figure out how to talk about what he had seen. He said: "You know, all the engineers and technical people who are astronauts, they just talk about things technically. I just didn't know any words for it."

In his speech, he used the second person, present tense—"Now you see this; now you see that." He said he did this because he realized that who he was as an astronaut was an *extension of the sensory organs of humankind.* "I was there," he said. "I could see something with my eyes, but it wasn't just me seeing. It was humankind seeing." So he tried to explain it. He said it helped him make sense of the experience in a different way: as both a collective experience that he shared with the world and as a way to see as another.

The latter part of that same speech is very moving:

Now you're near the end of the mission, and you're very fortunate because the mission has gone very well technically. And so you have free time that you really had no right to expect. So the last days you actually spend much of the time just looking out the window. And as you look out the window, you realize that your identity has shifted—that for the first several days, whenever you had the chance to look out the window, you looked for the west coast of California, or you looked for Texas, or you looked for the Florida peninsula. You looked for things that were familiar to you. And then you suddenly realize that you're now looking forward to the west coast of Africa. And you're looking forward to the Sinai. And you're looking forward to the Indian subcontinent. You realize that your identity has shifted, and you are now identifying with all of it.

And now you're well into the last day. And you find yourself just looking. And you're drifting over that very familiar piece of geography that we call the Middle East. And you're looking down at this, and suddenly it hits you that there are no boundaries. . . . You realize there are no lines. The lines only exist because we hold them in our mind as existing. Then you realize, at that instant, that people are busy killing each other over those imaginary lines.[2]

And that's where his talk ends.

A couple of years later Rusty participated in a three-day leadership course that our friend Peter Senge co-facilitated. At the end of the course, Peter invited him to say whatever he would like to say. He got up and told a little bit of the same story. Then Charlie Kiefer, the other facilitator, said, "So, Rusty, what was it like up there?" Rusty went silent and stood there for a long time, and then he said, "It was like seeing a baby about to be born."[3]

When we connect with that deeper place of stillness and awe and look at our planet now, in this moment, what can we sense that wants to be born? What is it on a planetary level? What is it on a personal level? What is it on the level of the social fields that we are co-sensing and co-enacting moment to moment? Our friend and colleague Arawana Hayashi likes to talk about the three bodies that we as human beings have to work with. They are (1) the big body, our planet; (2) the small body, our own physical body; and (3) our social body, the social field.[4] What does each one call us to pay attention to from moment to moment? The seven practices we described in the previous chapter are designed to help us figure this out. Each practice helps shift our mindset from the mode of the dog that chases the stick thrown in front of him to the mode of the lion that directs his attention to where the stick came from—to the source.

Navigating Roadblocks

The seed meditation sets the scene for the final part of our field walk. Let's begin by identifying three primary roadblocks to activating our real agency.

The first roadblock is the *illusion of insignificance*. We may think of ourselves as insignificant "grains of dust." But most transformations begin with, and are composed of, many small steps. One day in 2023 in the former East Berlin, we walked by a piece of the old Berlin Wall that was painted with graffiti, which read: "Many small people who in many small places do many small things can alter the face of the world." In 1989, that principle of distributed agency brought down the Berlin Wall. Today, many of us feel that the next big shift is just around the corner.

The second barrier to stepping into our agency is the hesitation to act in the face of *not-knowing*. Just because the future is unknown doesn't mean that we can't act. In fact, the U-process is organized around the opposite idea—namely, creating agency in the moment of disruption and stepping into the future *as it emerges*. Profound innovation and transformation can be compared to a hike. When on a hike, you need to know both where you want to go and where to take your next step, your next foothold. In situations of high emergence (and disruption), the same principles apply: you need a good sense of your direction (the power of intention), and you need to pragmatically figure out the next step. After taking this step, read the feedback that the universe is offering to you. It will tell you how to correct your course, adapt, and iterate. How do you read that feedback? Simply with your mind, but also with your heart. Your heart already knows.

The third barrier of course is fear. Recently, we had a live session with the participants of the 2024 u-lab. One question we asked was: "In a word or two, what is holding you back?" The number one answer that came up—and that always comes up—is *fear*. Fear is holding us back. How do we fight fear? By spelling out the worst case scenario (including how you would respond), and by focusing on what's most essential for you, on what you can't *not* do, then the whole thing about fear starts to fade more and more into irrelevance.

Three Options for Responding to the Polycrisis

All of us have seen amazing innovations and initiatives, small islands of coherence that created solutions but never managed to lift up an entire system. Individual innovators cannot shift the system by themselves. So the question remains: What does it really take to lift an entire system?

Our short answer is this: we need to *update* the *operating system*—meaning we need to upgrade how the different sectors of our society operate. Above the soil, the operating system consists of rules and protocols for each of the sectors and areas of society. But below the soil the operating system relies on eco-system leadership awareness and practices.

As mentioned earlier, there are three options that currently shape the political discourse of how to respond to the polycrisis of our time. The first one is more of the same, or *muddling through*. The results of muddling through are some new regulations that respond to the symptoms of the problem; these include some free-market solutions. Whatever has the public attention creates a quick response in the political sphere. In other words, we are merely firefighting the challenges.

The second option appears to be more radical. This response disrupts the status quo by focusing on *turning back*, making your home country "great again." Examples are calls for autocratic political structures and tech platform monopolies that concentrate all the economic or political power in the hands of a very few. This response can almost be described as a neofeudal structure of power (represented by the outer sphere in Foldout Color Plate 1).

The third option is not often part of mainstream political discourse, and it is also more radical than the status quo. This third option redirects the potential transformation in a different direction: *forward, into the emerging future.* Leaning forward means transforming the status quo not by exclusion, extraction, and control but by inclusion, regeneration, and partnership. This option is represented by the innermost sphere of the Wheel we refer to as 4.0.

Looking at election patterns around the world, there are three main take-aways. First, many or most people are rejecting the mere continuation of the status quo, muddling through with what already is. This trend, where incumbents tend to struggle, has persisted since the early twenty-first century. Second, people who want to see real change are willing to vote for populists even if they run platforms that include the undermining of democratic principles. And third, voters have rejected most movements toward autocratic structures. Yes, they may vote for populist candidates who promise real change. But if given the choice, they tend to reject the path toward autocracy.

This means that globally the majority of people largely agree that we need profound change and that we do not want to go back to autocracy and feudalism.

If both those things are true, why is the empirical response to the polycrisis mostly shaped by options 1 and 2? Because option 3, leaning into the future, is hard to do. It requires hard work. It requires profoundly new thinking that supports innovations, new ideas, and new practices. And it requires the courage to trust and step into an emerging vision of the future that could be transformational.

Deep Transitions and Transformations

As we learned from earlier historical shifts, like the collapse of the Berlin Wall, historical evolution and progress rarely follow a script. Instead, progress tends to unfold from complex situations with manifold players. Recall the strategy that Christiana Figueres deployed as the coordinator of the Paris climate negotiations. She combined two strategic tracks: bottom-up and top-down. She engaged institutional stakeholders (those at the "top") through deep listening and dialogue, and she launched "operation groundswell," its bottom-up complement for activating a movement from the ground up. These final two chapters explore both strategies.

We believe that leaning into the potential for the future calls for three important shifts:

- *shifting economies* from ego- to eco-systemic ways of operating;
- *shifting governance* toward a more distributed, dialogic, and direct way of operating; and
- *shifting learning and leadership* spaces to whole-person and whole-systems learning.

To achieve these three transformations calls for two forms of engagement. One is to act within our own direct sphere of influence and agency. This will be different for each of us. Some will work from within old but still significant and powerful structures such as institutions, helping to transform from within. Others will choose to work from the edges of the old system, co-creating inspiring living examples that prototype the new. Still others may focus on bridging, connecting, and cross-leveraging all these approaches.

The second is to attend to the transformation of the whole. The collective reality that we are perpetuating today is mainly a manifestation of yesterday's thinking about our economic, democratic, and educational systems. These are the foundations of society, and that's why change matters.

Each of us has a responsibility to turn the deep creative force that we are gifted with as humans—the power of our attention and intention—to shift the paradigm in these three key areas to 4.0. Because if we don't, it won't happen. *We grow in the direction of the attention and intention that we hold.*

Shifting Our Economies from Ego to Eco: Seven Acupuncture Points

Our economies are not static systems. They have evolved dynamically over time and continue to do so. Their gradual evolution can be described as an evolution of the operating system (OS). Like the operating systems on our electronic devices, once in a while they need an update. The difference is that to upgrade a device we just plug in and click "accept," while upgrading an economic system may take decades and involve significant struggles between new majorities and old special interests that want to preserve their existing privileges.

The way we frame our economic issues matters because it defines our everyday lives. How we think about the economy and the frameworks we teach in universities and business schools shapes our reality. It defines everything from institutional design to policy decisions. Our current economic reality is the embodiment of yesterday's economic thought. Today's economic thinking is shaping tomorrow's realities. The economy is at the core of today's societal structures. That is as true in the United States as it is in China. Even though contemporary governments usually have multiple ministries, most of them deal with the same meta-issue: the economy. All this is a long way of saying that the economy—and how we think about it—matters.

Shifting the economy and our economic frameworks from ego-system to eco-system thinking has very practical implications. Let's take as an example *nature*, an important "variable" in an economic production function. Does this frame consider nature to be a commodity or the living planet? The answer to this question will affect the policy recommendations that result.

Nature, labor, and capital are the three classical core production factors in economic theory. The main problem with this traditional approach, as pointed out by Karl Polanyi in his brilliant book *The Great Transformation*, is that nature, labor, and capital are treated as commodities in our current economic thinking.[5] He argues that commodities are only what we produce for and sell in the marketplace. But Mother Nature is not a commodity. She is a living ecosystem, or a living being. Human beings (labor) are not a commodity. They are living beings too. Our monetary system (capital) is not a commodity. For all these reasons, Polanyi coined the term *commodity fiction*.

Yet we treat these factors as commodities by trading land and labor in the market system. Even today all mainstream economic thought continues to defend this commodity fiction.

How have societies responded to issues created by this commodity? What has been the social response to the negative externalities of our economies? Societal movements formed and fought back. Farmers' associations, labor unions, and financial system regulators all shared the same objective: *suspend* the market mechanism and *redirect* collective agency by supplementing it with an arrangement that would better safeguard the well-being of the planet and its inhabitants.

That's where we are today. Over the past one hundred or so years, these 3.0 economic arrangements have produced massive economic progress, lifting hundreds of millions of people out of poverty. But the associated and considerable costs have become more and more evident: they are irreversible climate destabilization and biodiversity loss, as well as obscene levels of inequality within and between countries.

Now consider this question: What happens if we shift this ego-systemic way thinking to an eco-systemic way of thinking (labeled as the 4.0 economy in Figure 6.1). What would a 4.0 economy look like? What would it take to move beyond the old commodity fiction of nature, labor, capital, and technology in ways that serve human and planetary flourishing? Here are a few guiding questions for advancing that conversation:

Nature: How can we rethink our economic relationship with nature? Instead of "take, make, and waste," can we imagine an integrated closed-loop design, in which everything that we take from the Earth is returned to it at the same or a higher level of quality?

Labor: How can we relink work—the profession we choose to pursue—with our passion and purpose, what we really love doing? And how is it possible to make the opportunity to do that available to all?

Capital: How can we reestablish the link between the financial and the real economy? How is it possible to recycle financial capital to regenerate our ecological, social, and cultural commons?

Technology: How can we create broad access to the core technologies of the third Industrial Revolution (what we're in right now)? Can we devise ways to blend regenerative energy, social technologies, and AI that enhance (rather than diminish) awareness, creativity, and flourishing?

Leadership: How can we build a collective leadership capacity that co-senses whole systems and co-creates innovations that benefit everyone?

Consumption: How can we rebalance the economic playing field? Can we conceive of a system in which consumers and citizens can engage in conscious, co-creative consumption and become equal partners in an economy that works for all?

Governance: How can we update our governance system so that it links agency, impact, and accountability? Modern economies are based on a division of labor that requires a coordination process. Over the past several centuries, as social structures have differentiated into various semi-autonomous sectors, societies have developed three coordination mechanisms to address this challenge—and one emerging fourth one.

In an earlier book, we have outlined this shift in more detail.[6] In summary, there are four possible options for how to coordinate an economy:

- organize around a centralized power: the state sets the rules and calls the shots;
- organize around competition: the liberal market system;
- organize around stakeholder groups: the socially regulated market system; and
- organize around shared awareness and intention and utilize business as a force for good.

We are all familiar with the first three forms of coordinating an economy. They describe our current reality in different parts of the world. But the fourth coordination mechanism is an emerging form that exists all around us but does not yet have a name. When Patagonia, the outdoor clothing company, calls the Earth its only shareholder, when organic food goes mainstream, when farmers turn to CSA (community supported agriculture) as an operating model, we see innovations outside of the current economic model of 2.0 or 3.0.

We describe this as a shift from ego- to eco-system economies.

In an eco-system-oriented business, all decisions take into account what the eco-system needs.[7] That focus has huge implications for its operations, one of the most important of which is its relationship with its customers. Thomas Kuhn's work on scientific revolutions and Arnold Toynbee's work on the rise and fall of civilizations speak to our hopes for the next evolution of the economic paradigm.[8] Briefly, whenever an economic paradigm, or a system, is unable to provide useful answers to a period's biggest challenges, society will enter a transitional period during which, sooner or later, it replaces the existing logic and operating system with better ones.

What is the driving force for moving from one operating system to another? We believe that there are two primary ones, push and pull: a set of new exterior challenges (the push factor) that today comes in the form of our polycrisis, and the opening of a new awareness (the pull factor) that today comes in the form of an emerging planetary awareness. Societal evolutionary shifts happen when the forces of push and pull meet and align: a set of external challenges that can no longer be ignored aligns with the awakening of a new human consciousness and intention. In that spirit, take a moment to contemplate Figure 6.1, which outlines the evolution we have just described. Keep in

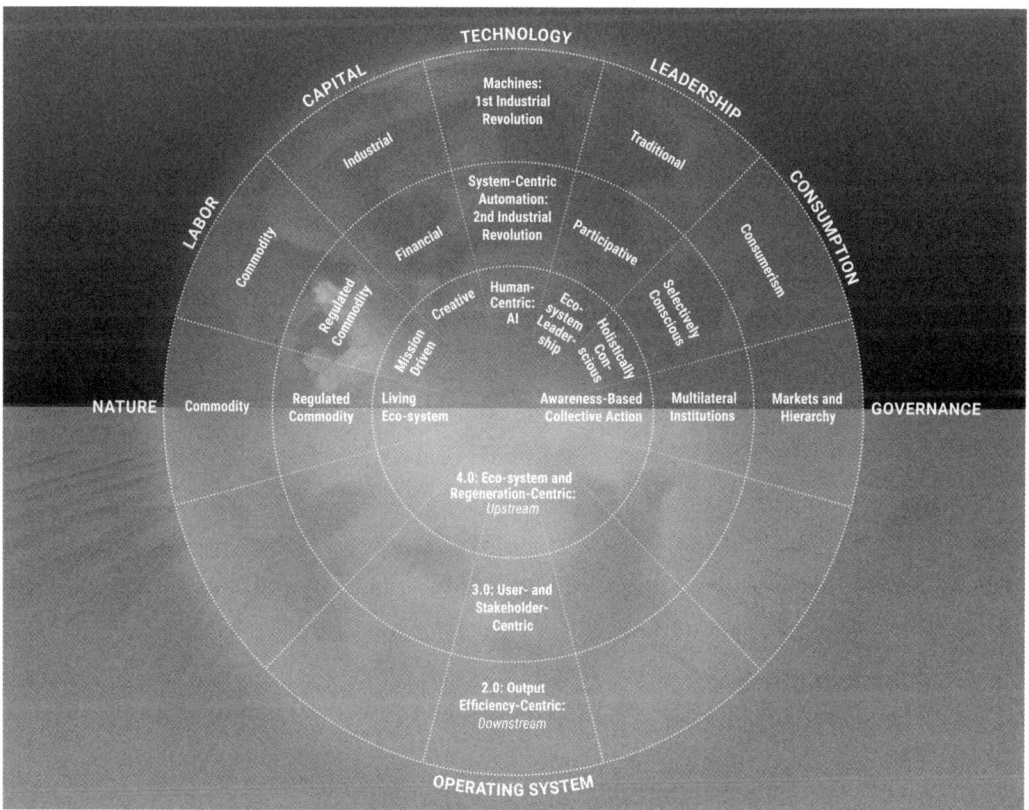

FIGURE 6.1: MATRIX OF ECONOMIC EVOLUTION

mind that the bigger trajectory of evolutionary forces described above relates to the bigger picture of the next few decades, not just to the next few years.

Shifting Democracies from Gridlock to More Dialogic, Distributed, and Direct Governance

Roughly two-thirds (69 percent) of the planet's population are willing to sacrifice part of their income to make progress on global issues like climate change. In the G20 countries three out of four people support the transformation of our economies to better address climate change and inequality.[9] But our current system of governance is unable to deliver on that. We don't know how to bridge the gap between what people want and how to do it.

Why? Our collective decision-making tends to be firmly in the grip of small but well organized special interest groups. For example, we provide massive subsidies for technologies that are causing climate change instead of taxing carbon. According to a 2023 International Monetary Fund (IMF) research update, fossil fuel subsidies were $7 trillion in 2022.[10] The same applies to agriculture. We subsidize industrial agriculture that degrades soil and water instead of paying farmers to speed up the transition to regenerative agriculture and support biodiversity, water preservation, and healthy food production. According to the World Bank Group, direct subsidies of $635 billion a year drive "the excessive use of fertilizers. . . . Subsidies for products such as soybeans, palm oil, and beef cause farmers to push into the forest frontier and are responsible for 14 percent of forest loss every year."[11] The Food and Agriculture Organization of the UN estimates that the hidden costs of our current agriculture system—expressed as its contribution to climate change, biodiversity loss, water scarcity and pollution, land degradation, poor nutrition, impact on future crop yields, and other areas—are approximately $12.7 trillion.[12] As if that's not enough, we continue with flawed foreign policy doctrines that benefit the military-industrial complex and that put the world at an irresponsible risk of a nuclear war. We retain tax loopholes and asymmetric tax arrangements that lower the effective tax rate the more one earns and that have led to a redistribution of wealth from the bottom 90 percent to the top 1 percent in the amount of roughly $50 trillion over the past fifty years.[13]

The gap between what most citizens want to see and the actual decisions of governments continues to widen. But that gap represents a powerful opportunity to upgrade our systems of governance.

Democracy Is in Retreat and under Attack

Our democracies are under attack. According to the Economist Intelligence Unit (EIU), the proportion of people living in democracies declined to 45 percent by 2023. Only 7.8 percent of the world's population lives in a "full democracy." It is noteworthy that the United States was demoted from a "full" to a "flawed democracy" in 2016. More than one-third of the world's population live under authoritarian rule (39.4 percent).[14] The Democracy Index, which is based on five indicators, has declined for all world regions. In 2023 the only region with a rising index was Western Europe, with the Nordic countries occupying four of the top five positions and New Zealand at number two. But that increase was very minimal. So, it's fair to say that the global state of democracy is stagnant and regressing.

The EIU notes that "even the world's most developed democracies are struggling to manage political and social conflict at home."[15] It seems that formal democratic institutions, the rule of law, and high standards of governance no longer enjoy undivided support, particularly among younger people. What this brings to our awareness is that any system of governance, democratic or otherwise, is based on *two* main sources of legitimacy. One is procedural (such as free and open elections). The other is measured in terms of actual outcomes. The rise of autocracy and the decline of democracy can be understood as an expression of frustration by large parts of the population, who believe that the current forms of governance ignore their needs or do not deliver on their promises.

The Evolution of Governance and Democracy

Democracy is not just a Western invention that originated in Greece. The roots of democracy, if understood as governance that works through consultation, dialogue, and consent, can be found in many early civilizations, including ancient China, Mesopotamia, Buddhist-era India, the tribal lands of the American Great Lakes, preconquest Mesoamerica, and precolonial Africa.

In the Western context, democracies also advance and recede in waves. The advances of the past two centuries have been an astonishing success. The ultimate sign of success is that today even autocratic rulers try to legitimize their rule by creating the appearance of democratic practices. In the West, this more recent democratic success story came in three waves. The first wave began in the late 1700s when voting rights were expanded to increasingly wider circles of citizens. The second wave began after World War II ended in 1945, in the context of decolonization. And the third wave began at the end of the Cold War in 1989, after the peaceful collapse of the Soviet Union.

Governance is essentially about the geometry of power. To evolve our democracy and governance systems in ways that make the widely shared aspiration for transformative change relevant for collective decision-making, we need to reduce the outsized impact that small vested interest groups wield. Their dominance stands in stark contrast to the underrepresentation of stakeholders without a voice, including future generations and our living planet.

If we extended eco-system governance to all of society's institutions, what would we see? We would work toward a unity of *agency, impact, and accountability.* Our colleague Kenneth Hogg, who has worked for the Scottish government for over thirty years, shared an example of when government begins to align these three factors. Kenneth organized a process of reform in the Scottish police service. He decided that, rather than government designing the change, the police forces themselves should design their ideal operating model. He asked them, if resources weren't a problem, what would your perfect solution be for Scotland? He initiated a process with the police and their stakeholders, including victims groups. One result of this process was a change of the statutory purpose of policing. The previous purpose had been "guard, patrol and watch." This purpose statement dated back to 1967, when the vision of policing was focused narrowly on preventing offending and "catching the bad guys."

Through the reform process this purpose changed to "improving the safety and well-being of people, localities and communities in Scotland." The suggestion came from within the police service. Says Kenneth:

> Promoting community well-being is a much broader vision than only catching criminals, and includes tackling the causes of offending. One of the things which the police service of Scotland has invested heavily in is training police officers in the impact of adverse childhood experiences (ACEs) and trauma-informed approaches to policing. Experiences like domestic violence can have multiple negative impacts on young people. Likewise, young people who have lived in the care system are overrepresented in later life amongst people who offend and who are victims of crime. It's remarkable that of all the public services in Scotland, apart of course from social work, the police service is now leading the way in these areas. To me that's an example of a public service questioning: What matters to us? What's our purpose? How do we engage upstream of the problems we deal with? How can we better serve our communities by promoting their well-being and the safety? How can we work better with other public services, like education, and health and social services, as part of the wider eco-system we work within? If we do that, we can tackle issues which will otherwise manifest years later as a much bigger problems.[16]

In a small community, unity of *agency, impact, and accountability* is relatively easy to achieve, but what if you are working on regional or global challenges? One possibility is innovating new institutions that form *arenas (spaces) for co-sensing and dialogue* among all the relevant players that would allow for *shared awareness and intention* to emerge in ways that can inform and guide collective agency *in sync* with that deeper intention, and not contrary to it.

The crisis of democracy calls for an update of democracy's operating system from

- a 1.0 one-party democracy (centralized, autocratic);
- to a 2.0 multiparty, indirect (parliamentary) democracy;

- to a 3.0 participatory, indirect (parliamentary) democracy; and finally,
- to a 4.0: direct, distributed, data-based, and dialogic (4D) democracy.

4D democracies are:

distributed: more decentralized and fluid, using technologies to advance democratic participation

data-driven: more informed by shared standards that provide relevant information and protect democracy against mass disinformation

dialogic: more open to both debate and dialogue—dialogue is a process of making systems see and sense themselves; to systematically strengthen dialogue across all institutions of governance requires a new set of institutional spaces that support pre-market and pre-regulation areas of co-sensing and eco-system governing

direct: more direct participation in the consultation and decision-making process of public governance; participation is more than just voting every four years—local and national-level citizen councils and referendums are good examples

These democracy-related practices have been cultivated in Indigenous communities for centuries. Today, however, the challenge is to use these principles and practices on a global scale. The more the old systems break down, the more we will see the emergence of 4D forms of democracy. They are already common in villages, in some urban areas, and wherever organizing occurs and a shared commons is valued.

The rise of citizen councils is another promising example of the rise of 4D practices. Citizen councils or assemblies convene citizens to deliberate on issues and make recommendations that can guide public policy. They began gaining attention in the late twentieth century as a way to address democratic deficits by involving citizens directly in decision-making processes. Initially prominent in Europe, particularly in Ireland and the United Kingdom, citizen assemblies have since been adopted by more than thirty countries worldwide. As of 2024, hundreds of such councils have been convened to address issues ranging from climate change to healthcare reform. For example, Ireland's Citizens' Assembly played a crucial role in the legalization of same-sex marriage and abortion.[17]

The organizers of these councils and assemblies, which provide the infrastructure, process, and facilitation for the change process, emphasize that their success depends not only on a sound structure and process (i.e., the tangible practices aboveground) but also the quality of convening, listening, and dialogue (i.e., practices related to the social soil).

Claudine Nierth, spokesperson for of the German NGO *Mehr Demokratie* (More Democracy), reflects on her experience: "Democracy is invisible unless we are enacting it. I have been fighting for years to ensure that we use it as widely and frequently as possible—in elections, referendums, and participation processes of all kinds. Having engaged with citizens and elected politicians on this for years, I have come to this realization: the higher the political office, the less room there is for maneuver. But where powerlessness is most strongly felt—among the citizens—is where the power and room for maneuver are greatest. Citizens don't have to make compromises, fight for a mandate, or withstand lobbying pressure."[18]

For Claudine, the ultimate leverage point for addressing our current polycrisis is democracy, which we must evolve and advance. "The independent freedom of citizens to shape things needs to be unlocked and leveraged. Politics improves when people are involved. In the years to come, we need to implement this principle all over the place."[19]

Shifting Learning from Transactional to Transformative

Updating our economic and democratic operating systems requires the creation of new collaborative spaces for sensemaking, for collective decision-making, and for innovating at the scale of the whole system. In other words, these transitions require new societal spaces that help to realign attention, intention, and agency at the level of the whole.

But, as many of you know from your own experience, new collaborative spaces are only fun and productive so long as you're dealing with people who aren't stuck inside their own silos. For these institutional innovations to work well, we need a profound upgrade of our learning and leadership structures—our schools, colleges, and universities. Without self-awareness and better listening and dialogue skills, our officials, teams, and leaders across sectors won't be able to co-navigate through the required transitions and challenges that are coming our way. Our institutions won't function at the level that we need them to. Education becomes a leverage point when, rather than updating "unlearn" and "relearn" ways of operating, these deeper collaborative and co-creative skills are integrated from the outset.

Figure 6.2 shows how mismatched our educational institutions are with the actual needs of our time. The primary focus of most of our current educational institutions is individual, mind-centric learning, while current best practices focus more on experiential forms of learning, or learning by doing. That's good, and it's real progress. But it's not enough.

Much of the most important and urgent learning needs are currently part of transformative learning—the top row in Figure 6.2. We refer to the significantly underserved space for learning in this figure as a "blind spot" in our current educational institutions. It is one of the most significant collective innovation challenges of our time. The advance of AI has only heightened the urgency of this challenge. The creation of the holistic folk high school in

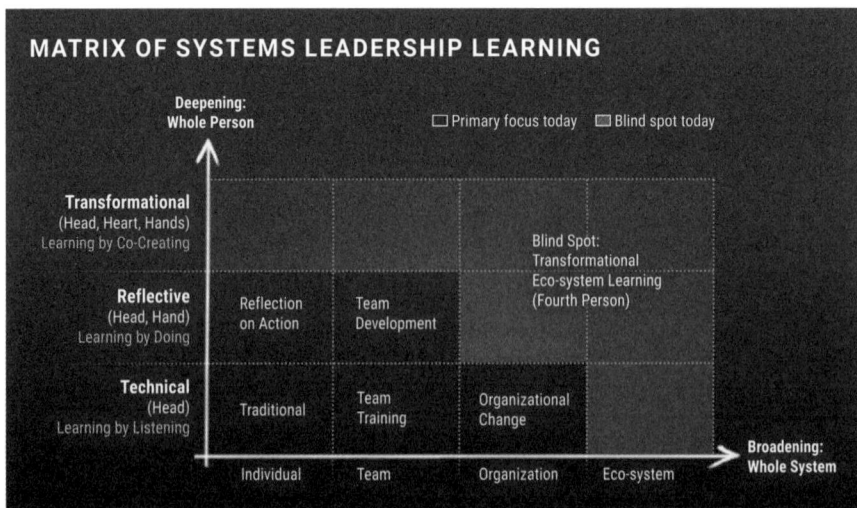

FIGURE 6.2: THE BLIND SPOT OF OUR EDUCATION SYSTEMS

nineteenth-century Denmark provided the infrastructure—the social soil—for the transformational innovation, growth, and flourishing that happened in the Nordic countries. How can we use that story as inspiration for reimagining our own educational systems—this time perhaps on a planetary scale?

In summary, the blind spot of our current educational system concerns the social soil. What would it take to illuminate that blind spot? Our learning environments are fertile ground for an upgrade in methods, practices, and holding spaces and a complementary core curriculum that develops a much-needed *transformation literacy*, or, in the language of the Wheel of Deep Change, the cultivation of the seven *eco-system leadership practices*: becoming aware, listening, dialogue, presencing, co-imagination, co-creation, and eco-system governance.

Figure 6.3 depicts the three transformations in the context of the Wheel of Deep Change:

- the seven acupuncture points for transforming our economies in the upper hemisphere;
- the seven core practices for transformation literacy in the lower hemisphere; and
- the evolution of democracy and governance can be thought of along the horizontal axis between governance and attention as the social soil (see also Foldout Color Plate 1).

The differentiation between the types of knowledge along the different spheres depicted in Figure 6.3 drives home another core point in this chapter: that the evolution of our learning and leadership institutions toward fourth-person knowing is an essential condition for the other transformations (depicted in the upper hemisphere) to succeed.

Pathways for Peace: Transforming Direct, Structural, Cultural, and Attentional Violence

The topic of war and peace is very close to our hearts as we both grew up in West Germany during the Cold War. I (Otto) later became an environmental and peace activist in both the West and the East. Later, as a student in Berlin, I was profoundly influenced by the thinking of Johan Galtung, who, inspired by the work of Mahatma Gandhi, became the founder of peace research as a science.

Around the world, the number of deaths in armed conflicts dropped to new lows during the 1990s and 2000s. But today some of the progress toward a more peaceful coexistence seems to be slipping away. Intrastate wars (state versus nonstate actors), nonstate conflicts (between nonstate armed groups, such as drug wars), and one-sided violent attacks (armed groups versus civilians) are increasing. Also, 2023 was the eighth year in a row that there have been more than fifty recorded state conflicts, and 2023 was the peak year with fifty-nine conflicts. The only other period since 1946 that there were over fifty conflicts in a year was in the early 1990s.[20]

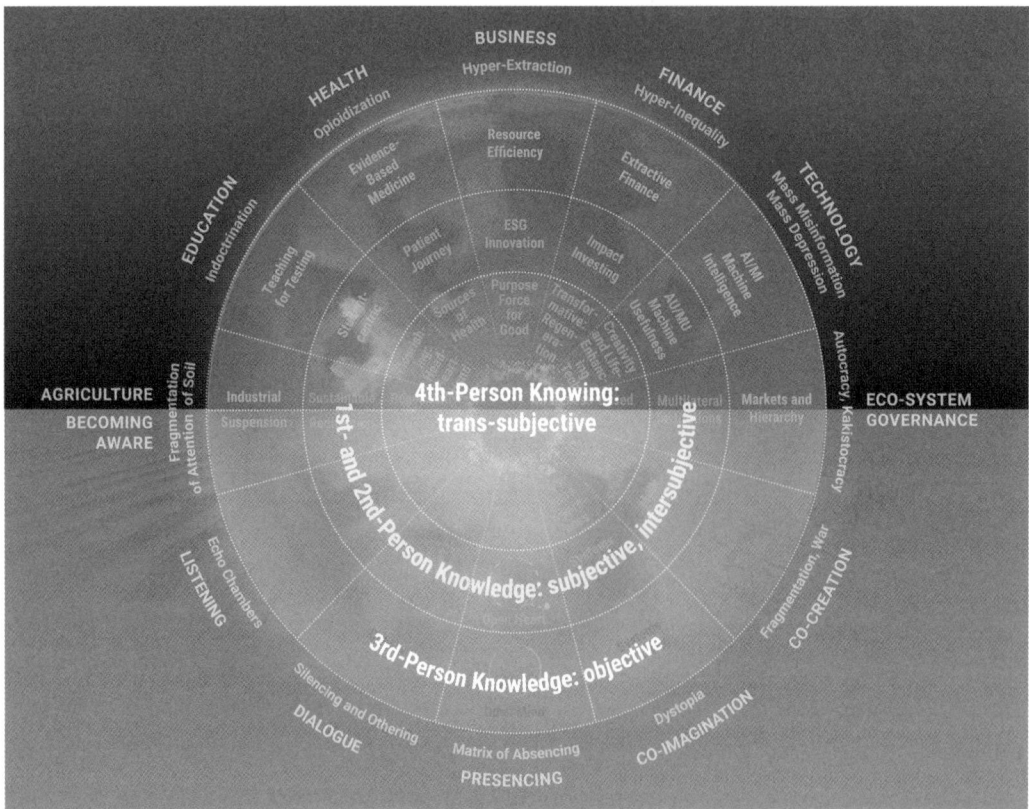

FIGURE 6.3: OPERATING SYSTEMS AND TYPES OF KNOWING

Many of today's conversations about war and peace feel like the "more of the same old thing"—we're spending more money on bombs and weaponry designed to kill mostly innocent civilians. Let us take a moment to use the Wheel of Deep Change to consider a different path forward.

First, looking at peace from the viewpoint of the top half of the Wheel, our key insight is that peace is not just the absence of violence. We need to think about a "positive peace" that allows all parties and stakeholders to co-shape the future they want.[21] This means that whatever issues are central to a conflict should not be narrowed but *broadened* (contrary to traditional approaches in diplomacy). Along with the primary two conflicting parties, additional players and stakeholders need to be involved. For example, in the Middle East, the site of one of the longest, most intractable conflicts of our time, could something like the Conference on Security and Cooperation in Europe (CSCE), established during and extended after the Cold War, be a path to a pact for shared prosperity and security?

Current policies in many parts of the world ignore the massive human, societal, and ecological destruction that war causes. *Positive peace* builds on engaging the whole *eco-system of players and partners* that need each other to transform the conflicts.

But what we see underlying many conflict zones, including the Middle East, can be described with a single word: kakistocracy—meaning rule by the worst. The result is a perpetuation of the cycle of violence, trauma, and more violence.

Yet we know that patterns can change, and even be transformed. There are plenty of historic examples. Before they became modern nation-states, France and Germany fought violent wars against each other for over a thousand years. But that pattern ceased to exist in 1945. The regime of warfare was replaced by cooperation toward shared prosperity—in other words, positive peace— through multilateral institutions that later became the European Union. The EU tends to be dismissed as bureaucratic by many both inside and outside of Europe, but in spite of its obvious shortcomings, it is a unique historical example of a structure of deep cooperation and multilateral integration at the regional-continental level that operates *without force by any hegemon*. It replaced negative peace with positive peace (at least inside EU territory).

What would it take to replicate, evolve, and adapt such a regionalization model in other parts of the world where it could be useful? That question brings us to our final point and shifts our focus to the less visible half of the Wheel, the social soil.

Galtung is known for developing the concept of *structural violence*. *Direct violence* describes a situation in which one person (the perpetrator) uses violence against another (the victim).

In the case of *structural violence*, no single person or group is the perpetrator. Instead, a collective arrangement excludes specific groups from fair access to opportunity. Systemic racism, sexism, and extreme poverty are examples. To understand peace and conflict only as matters of physical violence and counterviolence is to ignore less visible types of violence that inflict pain and suffering through other mechanisms.

In his later work, Galtung defined a third category of violence: *cultural violence*. Cultural violence points at assumptions and narratives that legitimate the use of violence in one way or another.

And, even less visible, is what Otto has called *attentional violence*: pain inflicted on people when they are not seen for who they really are and the potential they hold.

Much of our current diplomacy is still stuck on the first level or two. But truly transformative strategies for peace need to focus also on the deeper layers of violence, cultural and attentional, and begin to create small islands of coherence for positive peace by using all the relevant social soil practices to eliminate all forms of violence. That is exactly what the u-lab communities in Ukraine and in Israel and Palestine are working on. With the help of many others, they can continue by linking these islands to *eco-systems of coherence*. And then, as the old mindset of othering and brutal force clashes with reality, they can sense and seize opportunities for collaboration and positive peace as they emerge.

However, it is also evident how exhausting it is to hold this type of space for transformation and positive peace, which is exactly why a larger global community of people who want to support efforts toward positive peace is so much needed now.

Chapter 7

Protect the Flame

A ll areas of our society are faced with a polycrisis characterized by the continued degradation and destruction of our natural, social, and human eco-systems—in short—a *deepening* of the ecological, social, and spiritual *divides*. At the same time, we see *a story of regeneration* unfolding. That story is different from the one we learned in school and other traditional settings. It's a story about new ways of operating—what we have called 3.0 and 4.0 operating systems (OS). Instead of abstract efficiency, these new operating systems put users and stakeholders (OS 3.0) or the entire eco-system well-being and regeneration (OS 4.0) at the center. In agriculture, we see a transition from efficiency-focused industrial agriculture (the cause of almost half our environmental problems) to the production of organic food and *regenerative* agriculture. In education there is a movement away from teaching-for-testing and toward student-centered learning, and from there toward valuing *human flourishing*. Mission-driven businesses begin to transform their purpose and intention to operate as a *force for good*. In tech, there is a slowly growing awareness about how to use AI to *enhance awareness* and *creativity* rather than diminish it. The list goes on. Chapter 3 describes these and other transitions in more depth.

In other words, although most innovators and leaders think of their sectors as unique, they share many of the *same* problems and would benefit from the same kinds of solutions—not least because, as we saw in chapter 3, the issues of health and food or of finance, tech, and governance are not separate— they are one and the same and can only be addressed in a whole-systems approach. In simple terms, across all sectors we need to upgrade underlying operating systems. But facilitating such a deep systemic transition will be far from simple. This much-needed transition represents an enormous opportunity to create new spaces of societal innovation that support the regeneration and transformation of society, business, and self.

While the popular rhetoric supports moving from the old (2.0) to the new (4.0) ways of operating, actual change has been slow and at times even tends to backslide toward earlier stages. Traditional institutions are still in the firm grip of established habits and power structures. Many changemakers and leaders from major international institutions tell us, "We are trying to solve 4.0 challenges with 2.0 methods and tools" and "We are being encouraged to shoot for the moon while some of us are still driving a donkey cart."

Most citizens of the world say they support a transformation toward a regenerative way of living. Three out of four people in the G20 countries support transforming their economic systems to better address the challenges of inequality and climate change.

What would it take to bring people's desire for transformation into the mainstream? The key leverage point for advancing transitions from OS 2.0 to 4.0 has to do with the *social soil* that underlies everything we do. Like the farmer who cultivates the soil to enable crops to flourish, our individual and collective results are shaped by how we cultivate the social soil. Whether a hospital, a school, a business, or a startup operates in regenerative or extractive ways is largely a result of the *conditions of the social soil* that it exists within and that includes governance.

The seven practices for cultivating the social soil are outlined in chapter 5. The quality of the social soil influences the quality of the system, or how we live, work, and collaborate. When social media algorithms amplify misinformation and thus degrade our spaces for shared attention, listening, and dialogue, they threaten our democracies. If health, food, and education are treated as mere commodities, the planet and its people will continue to suffer.

Whether our highest future potential will become reality depends on our ability to cultivate the social soil. Because it isn't visible, it is often not acknowledged; but it remains the key to deep evolution in society and is crucial for our personal well-being.

Kindling the Flame

Accessing our highest potential has always been a hallmark of the human condition. It connects to the essence of our humanity, our inner flame. During his student days, Otto watched the artist Joseph Beuys accept the Wilhelm Lehmbruck Prize for sculpture in 1986. There he gave his last speech, shortly before his passing.

> Beuys spoke about the *flame of inspiration* Lehmbruck had provided for his entire artistic work. He closed his speech with the words, "Protect the Flame!"—*Schütze die Flamme!* These words struck a deep chord. In that moment I could suddenly feel how much that small flame, the essence of the human spirit, completely depends on all and on each of us, on people like Beuys who receive it, protect it, and then pass it on to the next generation. I felt as if in that moment I too had just received the flame, perhaps in a way similar to that Beuys did many years earlier.
>
> Protecting the flame is quite different from carrying or waving a torch. It is more like holding a candle in one hand and protecting the flame with the other—by holding the candle very close to your heart.

That may well be what is necessary today. Because our planet and well-being is already so fragile, each of us needs to protect the flame by holding it close to our heart. This will require an intentional support structure. No historical movement of transformation has ever succeeded without it. That support infrastructure must, among other things, democratize access to methods and tools of transformational leadership and learning.

Such a supporting infrastructure can have many faces. When in the nineteenth century the Nordic countries overcame poverty and isolation and transformed into progressive democracies focused on societal well-being, one driver of this transformation was the introduction of free "folk high schools," informal residential schools that provided learning opportunities in many subjects. Myles Horton, the founder of the Highlander Folk School in Tennessee, a key training center for US civil rights activists, including Dr. Martin Luther King, traveled to Denmark in the late 1920s to study the Danish folk high school model, particularly the schools developed by N. F. S. Grundtvig, and then adapted their principles to the context of racial and social justice in America. A support infrastructure does not have to be an educational institution. It can be an NGO, a business, or a public agency that cultivates a safe space for participants to reflect on their purpose and intention, to connect with others, and to acquire knowledge and skills.

This leads us to our final point. We founded the Presencing Institute to do exactly that: to prototype and experiment with support infrastructures that could be replicated and modified for any environment. Here we share a few important lessons that we have learned on our journey.

Moments of Collective Activation

In 2015 we launched a novel learning platform in collaboration with MITx—the u-lab. With our colleagues Adam Yukelson and Kelvy Bird, Otto spent nine months designing an eight-week learning journey, filming course videos, and building a platform through which participants could join peer coaching circles, self-organize into local "hubs" worldwide—co-shaped by our colleague Julie Arts—and go on a personal journey to connect with the future that needed them to emerge. The u-lab brought two things together that are usually separate: a scalable digital platform with low marginal costs (meaning that additional participants do not add costs to the program) and transformational learning experiences that included significant offline components.

When we launched, the response was overwhelming. Thirty-five thousand participants joined the first cohort, and the second cohort later in the same year drew more than forty-one thousand participants. It felt as if an entire global eco-system of dormant connections had been activated in an instant. After our first live session, in which we led a series of presencing practices, one posted on Twitter: "#Ulab This session brought me closer to my Self than previous 10 years of meditations, reading, occasional therapy and coaching! Thanks!"[1]

We initiated the global GAIA journey at the start of the Covid-19 pandemic (see chapter 5). In that moment of global disruption, Antoinette Klatzky and Otto, together with our Presencing Institute team and volunteers around the world, hosted biweekly online sessions to help people deal with the disruptions of the moment and think about profound societal transformation. We became an international "community" of about sixteen thousand, co-held by volunteers who translated conversations and material and co-facilitated sessions in seven languages. The infrastructure combined a high-quality holding space, inspiring content, personal reflection, social arts practices, and small-group work.

A third example of an enabling social infrastructure was created by our team in Latin America and shared in chapter 4. The in-person three-year Ecosystem Leadership Program (ELP) LATAM is designed to co-activate and support profound multi-local transformation. Its more than 250 participants include Indigenous elders, elected officials, business leaders, changemakers, social influencers, and grassroots activists from across the continent. The collective holding group has been deeply moved by the energy that is being activated through that incredibly diverse space and impressed by the over fifty prototype initiatives that the group has launched. These novel, large-scale, "crazy" gatherings are now possible. We call them "crazy" because they hold a deep space for transformation that can catalyze a profound shift in just a few days—which in our view suggests that these types of spaces are not only more needed but also a lot easier to create. Because most people feel that we live in moment of existential planetary risk and now is the time to come together and to lean into this situation with an open mind.

What do these three examples of social infrastructures for deep transformation have in common? Each one describes the activation of a generative social field based on Level 4 listening and dialogue that is at the creative inner core of the Wheel of Deep Change (Foldout Color Plate 1). Once that field is activated, it tends to feed on itself. As facilitators of these social infrastructures, we pay a lot of attention to how they begin, how we set the tone and intention, even to the inner preparation time before the official beginning. You start by establishing the quality of the social field—the levels of awareness, listening, dialogue, and sensing—using the tools and practices outlined in chapter 5.

On the Power of Social Arts

A critical backbone of all of our transformation support infrastructures are social arts–based *practice fields*, which allow participants to explore the seven core practices by experimenting with them in safe environments. The *social arts* are a backbone of awareness-based systems change because they provide powerful mechanisms for making a system see and sense itself. While there are many methodologies for making systems *see* themselves, there is a lack of rigorous methods for delivering on the *sensing* part of that foundation for consciousness-based systems change.

Social arts are sets of practices, drawn from various art forms, that support transformative learning by making visible the deeper structures of social systems: the *social soil*. As Arawana Hayashi, director and founder of Social Presencing Theater, comments, the word *theater* originates from the Greek verb *theastai*, which means "to behold." She comments, "Beholding is not a quick peek—a looking that bounces off the surface. One definition of the word behold is 'to gaze upon.' Beholding is relaxing the eyes, slowing down, attending, allowing resonance [or] a felt knowing to arise. It requires space. Beholding is seeing with the whole body, with an open heart. It enables a sense of deep connection and communication. Beholding holds the space for emergence, for what will appear, without judgment or opinion." This in-the-moment experience of the system at issue is key to moving from *systems thinking* to *systems sensing* and *systems presencing*.

And to do so we need innovations in social technologies, like social art practices, and in learning infrastructures. Social technologies, or awareness-based social technologies, are methods and tools that provide *transformation literacy*.

These methods, tools, and practices can be learned. Everyone possesses the seeds for these deeper capacities. But these seeds need practices to be activated. And to activate and develop them, we need spaces like those created by u-lab, GAIA, and ELP. The creation of these generative places operates by cultivating three connections:

- a *downward connection* to the land and earth that we feel in all our embodied structures, individually and collectively;
- a *horizontal connection* to the eco-system that we co-hold and co-evolve in our various contexts; and
- an *upward connection* to our highest future potential that depends on us to manifest.

Institutional Transformation

The examples like u-lab or GAIA given above describe how an eco-system is activated from the bottom up. These bottom-up activations need to be complemented with a set of institutional interventions—approaches that traditionally work from the top down.

A few years ago, we began working with the UN to develop a leadership workshop for teams implementing the UN's Sustainable Development Goals (SDGs) and working in crisis zones. This engagement was sparked by a conversation with Ifoda Abdurazakova, who worked for the UN in New York. We conceived the idea of a leadership lab that would help the siloed UN Country Teams to accelerate the implementation of SDGs and the Humanitarian

Country Teams to improve their response to humanitarian crises. A year later we held the first two prototypes of this lab, in Uganda and in Cambodia. Those successful workshops led to twenty-eight more SDG Leadership Labs in other countries.

Kenneth Hogg, program director and faculty member at the Presencing Institute, reflected on what he learned across all thirty SDG Labs: "The first learning that surfaced is that when trying to lead complex systems, top-down leadership won't work. This is not a new insight, but in these situations building the capacity for collaborative and co-creative leadership is critical for having the desired impact." Another key learning concerns purpose. "Very often . . . we find that leaders feel they have lost some of their connection with why they're doing the job. So, when we work with these leaders, we help them reconnect with a sense of purpose. Unless you are clear about your sense of purpose, I think it's almost impossible to lead impactfully."

Kenneth's third observation concerns listening. "The quality of listening directly impacts the capacity for action. This is one of the things that often is the most surprising to the participants in the SDG labs. Frequently they work for UN agencies or other organizations who are quite scientific in their approach. They see themselves as evidence-based organizations. It can be a surprise to them that the quality of their listening and of their dialogue can actually impact their capacity for action, for getting things done. They make the connection only over time; usually not initially." Kenneth continues:

Very often they initially question why we [encourage them to] suspend judgment and to pause, to set to one side some of the projects and the action plans, and to create a space to talk about things like quality of listening. And it's only once we go through the U-process that an appreciation emerges: yes, this thing I want to work on now, I didn't even feel that at the start of the program and now I sense a new opportunity. . . . Sometimes in the beginning, these leaders feel paralyzed by analysis. The labs introduce the idea of early prototyping, testing out at a very small scale in practice some new insights. And then rapid cycle learning to scale up. It generates that sense of freedom to explore things by experimentation and doing.[2]

u-school for Transformation

When systems collapse, what are we left with? We are left with each other, with the quality of our relationships to others, to ourselves, and to our planet. In other words, we are left with everything that makes up the social soil—the qualities of our awareness and relationships.

What Is Ours To Do? What Is It That We Can't Not Do?

Otto's father answered that question by making his life's work the cultivation of the soil and the community in and around the family farm. As he said, you cannot do one without the other. That belief led him and his family to transfer the private ownership of the farm to a steward ownership, with the planet as the only shareholder.

Our own response to the same question similarly focuses on the cultivation of the earth, but in our case, we focus on the *social soil*. To nourish that social soil, we need innovations in social and economic infrastructures. Like Otto's father, we believe that you can't do one without the other.

We are committed to creative commons and have made all tools and methods available through the non-profit Presencing Institute, which is dedicated to supporting the cultivation of the social soil. Our next major project in that context is a school without borders. This school will innovate and scale up supporting infrastructures that help changemakers across sectors and their organizations to cultivate the social soil.

When we co-founded the Presencing Institute with colleagues from across regions, our intention was to imagine and prototype a planetary multilocal support structure. We now call this platform the *u-school for Transformation*. Through this "school without borders" we will continue to innovate methods and tools for cultivating the social soil, democratize access to them, and demonstrate their impact through living examples.

This school without borders supports and nourishes the seeds of the future taking root in the form of manifold small islands of coherence and living examples. It connects these islands through infrastructures such as the u-lab or regional multiyear eco-system leadership programs; they support and amplify what is emerging. But the backbone of all of it is a global eco-system of small *circles of presence*, of holding spaces for supporting each other and protecting the flame of our and our planet's highest future potential.

We have prototyped *three building blocks* of this scalable infrastructure (Foldout Color Plate 2):

u-impact: empowering organizational and eco-system transformation by co-convening multistakeholder labs to foster mindset shifts and deliver practical, innovative solutions

u-research: advancing knowledge and practice by capturing key insights, developing innovative methods and tools, and sharing findings through books, articles, and our *Journal of Awareness-Based Systems Change.*

u-school: building the capacity to transform systems and self by democratizing access to the tools and practices of awareness-based systems change. Our goal is to empower change-makers to transform their systems by cultivating the social soil.

Although the impact of our work on the social soil is now slightly more visible, all this is just the beginning. The building blocks depicted in Foldout Color Plate 2 could be significantly scaled, localized, and/or adapted to sector-specific contexts (even though our social soil–focused approach happens to be in the blind spot of current philanthropic funding paradigms).[3]

Much of the positive emergence that we see across places can be powerfully amplified if the right kind of deep social change infrastructures are in place. The u-school for Transformation prototypes such support structures by cultivating the three source connections. Such an infrastructure will be powered by increasingly interconnected islands of coherence, a movement of changemakers across institutions and societal sectors that is connected to each other by a common purpose. Says our colleague Katie Stubley, senior faculty at the Presencing Institute: "We are not building the u-school, the u-school is building us."[4]

What If This Is the Very Moment That We Are Born For?

What if everything we have experienced in the past has prepared us for what is beginning now? What if the dormant movement begins to *see itself*? Such a process of *bending the beam of attention back* at the scale of the whole could profoundly shift the social field.

The question posed above—"What is mine to do?"—can't be answered once and for all. It's a question that we need to ask ourselves repeatedly, as circumstances change. In that spirit, we hope that the reflections and experiences we have shared here provide helpful context for your own reflections on this question. If this is the moment we are born for—what then is ours to do?

We deeply believe that now is the time to cultivate the soil for an emerging (un)movement—one that connects us all and nurtures the seeds of the future already present around us, between us, and within us, so they may take root, flourish, and guide us through this pivotal juncture and our journey ahead.

Presencing

Personal Reflection
and Dialogue Questions

1. What in this book resonates most with me?
2. What has shifted in my sense of self while reading this book?
3. Which of the seven social soil practices resonated most, and why?
4. Where in my life and work do I sense the seeds of the future?
5. How might one of those seeds grow into a small shoot. What might be possible if I dream forward?
6. Who are the three to five people who could support me in growing that seed?
7. How might the social soil practice that resonated with me the most be helpful to me now?
8. What is the most important intention that is crystallizing for me?
9. What support structures can help me to put this intention into practice (people, places, practices, platforms such as u-school.org, etc.)
10. What are some small, practical steps we can begin with?

For additional tools and practices, visit presencing.org.

Notes

Introduction

1 Martin Buber, *I and Thou* (New York: Scribner Classics, 2000).

2 Peter Senge, C. Otto Scharmer, Joseph Jaworski, and Betty Sue Flowers, *Presence: Human Purpose and the Field of the Future* (Cambridge, MA: SoL Press, 2004); C. Otto Scharmer, *Theory U: Leading from the Future as It Emerges* (San Francisco: Berrett-Koehler, 2009; 2nd ed. 2016). See also C. Otto Scharmer and Katrin Kaufer, *Leading from the Emerging Future: From Ego-System to Eco-System Economies* (Oakland, CA: Berrett-Koehler, 2013; 2nd ed. 2016).

3 Buber, *I and Thou*, 89.

4 Otto Scharmer and Eva Pomeroy, "Fourth Person: The Knowing of the Field," *Journal of Awareness-Based Systems Change* 4, no. 1 (2024): 19–48, https://doi.org/10.47061/jasc.v4i1 .7909.

5 "Transcript: Dr. Báyò Akómoláfé on Ontological Mutiny," *For the Wild*, podcast #338, with Ayana Young, June 30, 2023, https://forthewild.world/podcast-transcripts/dr-bayo-akomolafe -on-ontological-mutiny-338.

6 We thank our colleague Laura Pastorini for pointing out that attentional violence is distinct from cultural violence.

CHAPTER 1

1 *Breaking the Gridlock: Reimagining Cooperation in a Polarized World*, Human Development Report 2023–24 (United Nations Development Programme, 2024), 7, https://hdr.undp.org/content/human-development-report-2023-24.

2 "Expanding Agency for Collective Action," chap. 5 in *Breaking the Gridlock*.

3 "Agency Gaps in Collective Action Are Higher Than Those in Control Over One's Own Life," *Breaking the Gridlock*, figure S.7, 9.

4 "74 Percent of People in G20 Want Economic Transformation," Earth4All, August 18, 2021, https://earth4all.life/news/74-of-people-in-g20-want-economic-transformation/.

5 Thích Nhất Hạnh, "Clouds in Each Paper," Awakin, accessed August 29, 2024, https://www.awakin.org/v2/read/view.php?tid=222.

6 "u-lab: Leading from the Emerging Future," MITx Online, accessed August 29, 2024, https://mitxonline.mit.edu/courses/course-vi:MITxT+15.671.1x/.

CHAPTER 2

1 C. Otto Scharmer, *Theory U: Leading from the Future as It Emerges* (San Francisco: Berrett-Koehler, 2009; 2nd ed. 2016).

2 Donella H. Meadows et al., *The Limits to Growth: A Report for the Club of Rome's Project on the Predicament of Mankind* (New York: Universe Books, 1972).

3 Sandrine Dixson-Declève, "Another World Is Possible. But We Need More Ambitous Action by Governments. First Stop: Stockholm+50," Earth4All, May 23, 2022, https://earth4all.life/views/dixson-decleve-stockholm50/.

4 Jamie Bristow et al., *The System Within: Addressing the Inner Dimensions of Sustainability and Systems Transformation* (Earth4All Deep-Dive Paper 17, May 2024), https://www.clubofrome.org/wp-content/uploads/2024/05/Earth4All_Deep_Dive_Jamie_Bristow.pdf.

5 C. Otto Scharmer, *The Essentials of Theory U: Core Principles and Applications* (Oakland, CA: Berrett-Koehler, 2018), 87.

6 Dayna Cunningham, personal communication, June 2024.

CHAPTER 3

1 Jessica Y. Ho, "Life Course Patterns of Prescription Drug Use in the United States," *Demography* 60, no. 5 (2023): 1549–79, https://doi.org/10.1215/00703370-10965990.

2 Keiter, *Industry Report: US Nonprofit Sector*, January 2, 2024, https://keitercpa.com/wp-content/uploads/NFP-Industry-Report_2024.pdf; Bureau of Economic Analysis, "News Release:

Gross Domestic Product, Fourth Quarter and Year 2023 (Advance Estimate)," January 25, 2024, https://www.bea.gov/news/2024/gross-domestic-product-fourth-quarter-and-year-2023-advance -estimate; https://www.visualcapitalist.com/visualizing-u-s-gdp-by-industry-in-2023/; https:// usafacts.org/answers/how-much-does-the-us-federal-government-spend/country/united-states/.

3 One example are banks that are members of the GABV.

4 Daron Acemoglu and Simon Johnson, "Big Tech Is Bad. Big A.I. Will Be Worse," *New York Times*, June 9, 2023.

5 Personal conversations, June 2024.

6 Personal conversations, June 2024.

7 John Dewey, *The Public and Its Problems: An Essay in Political Inquiry*, ed. Melvin L. Rogers (University Park: Pennsylvania State University Press, 2012).

8 "About B Corp Certification: Measuring a Company's Entire Social and Environmental Impact," B Lab, accessed September 2024, https://www.bcorporation.net/en-us/certification/.

9 Becky Buell, personal conversation, September 2024.

10 Personal conversations, June 2022.

11 Thích Nhất Hạnh, "The Sutras on Dependant Co-Arising and Great Emptiness," Dharma Talk given by Thích Nhất Hạnh on March 19, 1998, Plum Village, France, http://www .abuddhistlibrary.com/Buddhism/G%20-%20TNH/TNH/The%20Sutras%20on%20Depen-dent%20Co-arising%20and%20Great%20Emptiness/Dharma%20Talk%20given%20by%20 Thich%20Nhat%20Hanh%20on%20March%2019.htm.

12 Marian Goodman, personal conversation, June 17, 2024.

13 Shoshana Zuboff, "Caveat Usor: Surveillance Capitalism as Epistemic Inequality," in *After the Digital Tornado: Networks, Algorithms, Humanity*, ed. Kevin Werbach (Cambridge: Cambridge University Press, 2020), 174–214. An open access copy of the chapter is available at https://www.cambridge.org/core/books/after-the-digital-tornado/caveat-usor-surveillance -capitalism-as-epistemic-inequality/9EB949FA5BD07CF448C7D8F6A226B975

14 Carter C. Price and Kathryn A. Edwards, *Trends in Income from 1975 to 2018*, Working Paper WR-A516-1 (RAND Corporation, September 14, 2020), https://www.rand.org/pubs /working_papers/WRA516-1.html.

15 *Breaking the Gridlock* (United Nations Development Programme, 2024), 7, https://hdr .undp.org/content/human-development-report-2023-24.

CHAPTER 4

1 Martin Buber, *I and Thou* (New York: First Scribner Classic Edition, 2000), 65.

2 Joseph Campbell, *The Hero with a Thousand Faces*, 3rd ed. (Novato, CA: New World Library, 2008).

3 Eva Pomeroy and Keira Oliver, "Action Confidence as an Indicator of Transformative Change," *Journal of Transformative Education* 19, no. 1 (2021): 68–86, https://doi.org/10.1177/1541344620940815.

4 "Three Gestures of Becoming Aware: Conversation with Francisco Varela," interview by Otto Scharmer, *Transformation Dialogues*, u-school for Transformation by the Presencing Institute, Paris, France, January 12, 2000, https://pi-2022.s3.amazonaws.com/doc_varela_2000_32d1683924.pdf.

5 "Three Gestures of Becoming Aware," 4.

6 Edgar H. Schein, *Humble Inquiry: The Gentle Art of Asking Instead of Telling* (Oakland, CA: Berrett-Koehler, 2013), 13.

7 "Address to the Nation by Nelson Mandela on the Assassination of Chris Hani," April 13, 1993, http://www.mandela.gov.za/mandela_speeches/1993/930413_hani.htm.

8 "Summary of Findings," Watson Institute for International & Public Affairs, accessed November 10, 2024, https://watson.brown.edu/costsofwar/papers/summary.

9 "About UID," United in Diversity, accessed November 9, 2024, https://unitedindiversity.org.

10 Frans Sugiarta, personal conversation, July 24, 2024.

11 Sugiarta, personal conversation, July 24, 2024.

12 The ELP LATAM Core Team consists of Becky Buell, Carolina da Rosa, Dayani Centeno, Florencia Estrade, Janine Saponara, Mariana Miranda, and Viviana Galdames. They are supported by Adriana Canales, Andrea Fernández, Daniela Ferraz, Geisa Paganini, Magali Meneses, and Sebastian Jung, and the generous work of all of the local volunteers in Uruguay, Chile, and Mexico (coming soon).

13 Laura Pastorini, personal conversation, July 2024.

14 Laura Pastorini, personal conversation, July 2024.

15 The original GAIA team and later Teoría U en Español included Helio Borges, Edinson Castaño, Dayani Centeno, Andrea Fernández, Viviana Galdames, Antonio Moya, Elizabeth Pérez, Vivianna Rodríguez, and Mónica Sulecio, among others.

16 Br Pháp Hữu and Jo Confino, "Being the Change We Want to See in the World: A Conversation with Christiana Figueres," *The Way Out Is In* podcast, episode 21, February 16, 2022, https://plumvillage.org/podcast/being-the-change-we-want-to-see-in-the-world-a-conversation-with-christiana-figueres-episode-21.

17 For a full transcript of Christiana Figueres's reflections, see Br Pháp Hữu and Jo Confino, "Being the Change We Want to See in the World," *The Way Out Is In* podcast, https://plumvillage.org/podcast/being-the-change-we-want-to-see-in-the-world-a-conversation-with-christiana-figueres-episode-21.

18 "RR Leadership for Awareness-Based Systems Transformation: Workshop 4 (Presencing)," posted April 27, 2022, by SparkBlue, YouTube, https://www.youtube.com/watch?v=9LiNRwSY5xA.

19 Otto Scharmer and Eva Pomeroy, "Fourth Person: The Knowing of the Field," *Journal of Awareness-Based Systems Change* 4, no. 1 (2024): 19–48, https://doi.org/10.47061/jasc.v4i1 .7909.

20 Mihaly Csikszentmihalyi, *Flow: The Psychology of Optimal Experience* (New York: Harper & Row, 1990).

21 Bill Russell and Taylor Branch, *Second Wind: The Memoirs of an Opinionated Man* (New York: Random House, 1979).

22 Eva Pomeroy, personal conversation, August 27, 2024.

23 Eleanor Rosch, "Primary Knowing: When Perception Happens from the Whole Field," interview by Otto Scharmer, Transformation Dialogues, u-school for Transformation by the Presencing Institute, October 15, 1999, 19, https://pi-2022.s3.amazonaws.com/doc_rosch _1999_8127312394.pdf.

24 Karl Jaspers, *The Origin and Goal of History*, trans. Michael Bullock (New Haven, CT: Yale University Press, 1953).

25 Francisco J. Varela, Eleanor Rosch, and Evan Thompson, *The Embodied Mind: Cognitive Science and Human Experience* (Cambridge, MA: The MIT Press, 1992).

26 Claire Petitmengin, "Describing One's Subjective Experience in the Second Person: An Interview Method for the Science of Consciousness," *Phenomenology and the Cognitive Sciences* 5 (2006): 229–269, https://doi.org/10.1007/s11097-006-9022-2.

27 "Eleanor H. Rosch," UC Berkeley Psychology, accessed September 1, 2024, https:// psychology.berkeley.edu/people/eleanor-h-rosch.

28 Camilla Valenzuela-Moguillansky, "Publications in Constructivist Foundations," Con-structivist Community, https://constructivist.info/authors/camila-valenzuela-moguillansky.

29 Nan Huai-Chin, *Basic Buddhism: Exploring Buddhism and Zen* (Newbury Port, MA: Weiser Publisher, 1997).

30 Melanie Goodchild, "Relational Systems Thinking: That's How Change Is Going to Come, from Our Earth Mother," *Journal of Awareness-Based Systems Change* 1, no. 1 (2021): 75–103, https://doi.org/10.47061/jabsc.v1i1.577.

31 Tyson Yunkaporta, *Right Story, Wrong Story: Adventures in Indigenous Thinking* (Mel-bourne: Text Publishing, 2023).

32 Robin Wall Kimmerer, *Braiding Sweetgrass: Indigenous Wisdom, Scientific Knowledge, and the Teachings of Plants* (Minneapolis, MN: Milkweed Editions, 2013).

33 Báyò Akómoláfé's website: https://www.bayoakomolafe.net.

34 Martin Kalungu-Banda, with Mbololwa Kalungu-Banda, *Driftology: How to Access Life's Greatest Opportunities by Flying on the Wings of Others* (Bloomington, IN: Authorhouse, 2015).

35 Arawana Hayashi and Ricardo Dutra, *Social Presencing Theater: The Art of Making a True Move* (Cambridge, MA: Pi Press, 2021).

36 Kelvy Bird, *Generative Scribing: A Social Art of the 21st Century* (Cambridge, MA: Pi Press, 2018).

37 Jon Kabat-Zinn, *Wherever You Go, There You Are: Mindfulness Meditation in Everyday Life* (New York: Hachette Books, 2005).

38 Daniel Goleman, *Emotional Intelligence: Why It Can Matter More Than IQ* (New York: Bantam Books, 2020).

39 Peter M. Senge, *The Fifth Discipline: The Art and Practice of the Learning Organization* (New York: Doubleday, 1990); C. Otto Scharmer, *The Essentials of Theory U: Core Principles and Application* (San Francisco: Berrett-Koehler, 2018).

40 Scharmer and Pomeroy, "Fourth Person."

41 Edgar H. Schein, *Humble Inquiry: The Gentle Art of Asking Instead of Telling* (San Francisco: Berrett-Koehler, 2013).

42 Johann Wolfgang von Goethe, *The Metamorphosis of Plants*, trans. Douglas Miller (Cambridge, MA: The MIT Press, 2009).

43 Edmund Husserl, *Ideas: General Introduction to Pure Phenomenology*, trans. W. R. Boyce Gibson (New York: Routledge, 2012).

44 Humberto R. Maturana and Francisco J. Varela, *The Tree of Knowledge: The Biological Roots of Human Understanding*, rev. ed. (Boston, MA: Shambhala, 1992); "Love: Letting Appear—Humberto Maturana & Otto Scharmer—Insightful Conversation," posted June 21, 2020, by Bridging Foundations for a LiveAble Future, YouTube, https://www.youtube.com/watch?v=Q4gNRiQuEQo.

45 Donella H. Meadows, Jorgen Randers, and Dennis Meadows, *Limits to Growth: The 30-Year Update* (White River Junction, VT: Chelsea Green Publishing, 2004).

46 Arthur Zajonc, *Meditation as Contemplative Inquiry: When Knowing Becomes Love* (Great Barrington, MA: Lindisfarne Books, 2009).

47 Senge, *The Fifth Discipline.*

48 Goodchild, "Relational Systems Thinking."

49 Goodchild, "Relational Systems Thinking," 99.

50 Melanie Goodchild, "Relational Systems Thinking: The Dibaajimowin (Story) of Re-Theorizing 'Systems Thinking' and 'Complexity Science,' *Journal of Awareness-Based Systems Change* 2, no. 1 (2022): 53–76, https://doi.org/10.47061/jabsc.v2i1.2027. Quote on p. 71.

51 Joanna Macy and Jess Serrante, *We Are the Great Turning* podcast, episode 10, June 20, 2024, https://resources.soundstrue.com/podcast/s1-ep-10-we-are-the-great-turning/; https://drive.google.com/file/d/16oy-DN4QDnGKsI5vMzQB74VXuHOoVGIF/view.

52 Pomeroy, personal conversation, August 27, 2024.

53 Schein, *Humble Inquiry.*

Chapter 5

1 Lene Rachel Andersen and Tomas Björkman, *The Nordic Secret: A European Story of Beauty and Freedom* (Copenhagen: Fri Tanke, 2017).

2 Laura Pastorini, personal communication, June 24, 2024.

3 C. Otto Scharmer, *The Essentials of Theory U: Core Principles and Application* (San Francisco: Berrett-Koehler, 2018), 34.

4 We owe this example to Arawana Hayashi (personal conversation). See also Dilgo Khyentse Rinpoche, "Be Like a Lion," Just Dharma: Celebrating Truth, accessed September 1, 2024, https://justdharma.org/be-like-a-lion/.

5 "Eileen Fisher on Why We Need Eachother," Women Together, accessed September 1, 2024, https://womentogether.com/lifenotes/article/eileen-fisher-on-why-we-need-each-other/.

6 "Our Tools," u-school for Transformation, accessed November 10, 2024, https://www.u-school.org/resources.

7 Kelvy Bird, *Generative Scribing: A Social Art of the 21st Century* (Cambridge, MA: Pi Press, 2018), 77.

8 Manish Srivastava, personal conversation, July 24, 2024. Lightly edited for clarity.

9 "Empathy Walk," u-school for Transformation by the Presencing Institute, accessed September 1, 2024, https://www.u-school.org/empathy-walk.

10 "Case Clinic," u-school for Transformation by the Presencing Institute, accessed September 1, 2024, https://www.u-school.org/case-clinic.

11 Personal conversation in 2022.

12 "Märkisches Landbrot: Der Runde Tisch Getreide," accessed September 1, 2024, https://archiv.landbrot.de/aktuelles/oeffentlichkeit/neuigkeiten/detail/article/runder-tisch-getreide-2023.html.

13 Julie Arts, personal conversation, July 26, 2024. Lightly edited for clarity.

14 William Isaacs, *Dialogue: The Art of Thinking Together* (New York: Doubleday Press, 1999).

15 "Container Building," u-school for Transformation by the Presencing Institute, accessed September 1, 2024, https://www.u-school.org/container-building.

16 Isaacs, *Dialogue*.

17 Marian Goodman, personal conversation, July 14, 2024. Lightly edited for clarity.

18 Vanesa Weyrauch, personal conversation, May 2024. Lightly edited for clarity.

19 "The Nova Scotia Quality of Life Initiative," Engage Nova Scotia, accessed September 1, 2024, https://engagenovascotia.ca/about-qol.

20 Danny Graham, personal conversation, July 4, 2024. Lightly edited for clarity.

21 "When We Know Better, We Do Better," Engage Nova Scotia, accessed September 1, 2024, https://engagenovascotia.ca/engaging-stories-wellbeing-blog/when-we-know-better-we-do-better.

22 Goodman, personal conversation, July 14, 2024.

23 Bird, *Generative Scribing.*

24 "GAIA Journey," u-school for transformation by the Presencing Institute, accessed September 1, 2024, https://www.u-school.org/offerings/gaia-recordings.

25 Antoinette Klatzky, personal conversation, September 2024.

26 Laura Pastorini, personal conversation June 2024.

27 "Colectivo Ciudadano de Unidad y Acción," Querétaro es Uno, accessed September 1, 2024, https://www.queretaroesuno.org/.

28 Willy Azarcoya, personal conversation, August 19, 2024. Lightly edited for clarity.

29 "First Stage," Querétaro es Uno, accessed October 3, 2024, https://www.queretaroesuno.org/np-conoce-qes1/.

30 Scharmer, *The Essentials of Theory U*; Peter Senge et al., *Presence: Human Purpose and the Field of the Future* (New York: Crown Currency, 2008); C. Otto Scharmer, *Theory U: Leading from the Future as it Emerges* (Oakland, CA: Berrett-Koehler Publishers, 2009; 2nd ed. 2016).

31 Johan Wolfgang von Goethe, *Faustus, A Dramatic Mystery*, trans. John Anster (London: Green & Longman, 1835), 15 (emphasis added).

32 For more information on this activity, visit https://www.u-school.org/seeds.

33 Arawana Hayashi and Ricardo Dutra, *Social Presencing Theater: The Art of Making a True Move* (Cambridge, MA: Pi Press, 2021).

34 Mikaela Weisse and Liz Goldman, "Primary Rainforest Destruction Increased 12% from 2019 to 2020," Global Forest Review, World Resources Institute, March 8, 2021, https://research.wri.org/gfr/global-tree-cover-loss-data-2020.

35 Silverius Oscar Unggul, personal conversation, June 2024. Lightly edited for clarity.

36 Silverius Oscar Unggul, "Brief Remarks from Telapak's President: Turning a Catastrophe into Hope," Telapak website, accessed June 2024, https://www.telapak.org/about-us/telapaks-story/.

37 Unggul, personal conversation, June 2024. Lightly edited for clarity.

38 "An Advancement of Community Development Towards Sustainable Livelihoods," Telapak, accessed September 1, 2024, https://www.telapak.org/.

39 GLS Bank, "Social Design through Visions of the Future," accessed September 1, 2024, https://nachhaltigkeitsbericht2022.gls.de/wie-dein-geld-wirkt/.

40 For more information on this tool, visit https://www.u-school.org/prototyping.

41 "People Finding Better Ways Forward," Innovators Compass, accessed September 1, 2024, https://innovatorscompass.org/.

42 Bambang Supriyanto and Yuli Prasetyo, personal conversation, January 29, 2024.

43 Bambang Supriyanto, personal conversation, May 2024. Lightly edited for clarity.

44 Supriyanto and Prasetyo, personal conversation, January 29, 2024. Lightly edited for clarity.

Chapter 6

1 Attributed to Rudolf Steiner.

2 Quoted in C. Otto Scharmer, *Theory U: Leading from the Future as it Emerges* (Oakland, CA: Berrett-Koehler Publishers, 2009; 2nd ed. 2016), 345.

3 Quoted in Scharmer, *Theory U*, 346.

4 Arawana Hayashi and Ricardo Dutra, *Social Presencing Theater: The Art of Making a True Move* (Cambridge, MA: Pi Press, 2021), 123.

5 Karl Polanyi, *The Great Transformation: The Political and Economic Origins of Our Time* (New York: Rinehart, 1944).

6 C. Otto Scharmer and Katrin Kaufer, *Leading from the Emerging Future: From Ego-System to Eco-System Economies* (Oakland, CA: Berrett-Koehler, 2013).

7 Katrin Kaufer and Lillian Steponaitis, *Just Money: Mission-Driven Banks and the Future of Finance* (Cambridge, MA: MIT Press, 2022).

8 Thomas S. Kuhn, *The Structure of Scientific Revolutions*, 3rd ed. (Chicago: University of Chicago Press, 1996); Arnold Toynbee, *A Study of History* (Oxford: Oxford University Press, 1963).

9 "74% of People in G20 Want Economic Transformation," Earth4All, August 18, 2021, https://earth4all.life/news/74-of-people-in-g20-want-economic-transformation/.

10 Simon Black, Antung A. Liu, Ian W. H. Parry, and Nate Vernon, *IMF Fossil Fuel Subsidies Data: 2023 Update*, IMF Working Paper No. 2023/169, August 24, 2023, https://www.imf.org/en/Publications/WP/Issues/2023/08/22/IMF-Fossil-Fuel-Subsidies-Data-2023-Update-537281.

11 "Trillions Wasted on Subsidies Could Help Address Climate Change," World Bank Group, June 15, 2023, https://www.worldbank.org/en/news/press-release/2023/06/15/trillions-wasted-on-subsidies-could-help-address-climate-change.

12 "Hidden Costs of Agrifood Systems at the Global Level," The State of Food and Agriculture 2023, Food and Agriculture Organization of the United Nations, accessed September 2024, https://openknowledge.fao.org/server/api/core/bitstreams/8a80e31b-3c41-419d-a11d-0b62e4b2528a/content/state-of-food-and-agriculture-2023/hidden-costs-global-level.html.

13 Price and Edwards, *Trends in Income from 1975 to 2018*.

14 "Democracy Index 2023: Age of Conflict," Economist Intelligence Unit, accessed September 2024, https://pages.eiu.com/rs/753-RIQ-438/images/Democracy-Index-2023-Final-report.pdf.

15 "Democracy Index 2023," 4.

16 Kenneth Hogg, personal conversation, August 14, 2024.

17 For definitions of citizens assemblies and more information on the Citizens' Assembly of Ireland, visit https://www.citizensinformation.ie/en/government-in-ireland/irish-constitution-1/citizens-assembly/.

18 Claudia Nierth, personal conversation, August 17, 2024.

19 Nierth, personal conversation, August 17, 2024.

20 "New Data Shows Record Number of Armed Conflicts," Peace Research Institute Oslo (PRIO), June 10, 2024, https://www.prio.org/news/3532.

21 Johan Galtung, *Peace by Peaceful Means: Peace and Conflict, Development and Civilization* (Thousand Oaks, CA: Sage Publications, 1996); Johan Galtung, "Violence, Peace, and Peace Research," *Journal of Peace Research* 6, no. 3 (1969): 167–91.

Chapter 7

1 Markéta Kunešová. (@sumpermarket76), "This session brought me closer to my Self than previous 10 years of meditations, reading, occasional therapy and coaching! Thanks!" Twitter (now X), January 28, 2015, https://twitter.com/supermarket76/status/560476796790263808?ref_src=twsrc%5Etfw.

2 Kenneth Hogg, personal conversation, August 14, 2024.

3 Otto Scharmer, "Philanthropy 4.0: Giving in Times of Disruption," Field of the Future Blog, *Medium,* December 21, 2023, https://medium.com/presencing-institute-blog/philanthropy-4-0-what-form-of-giving-enables-transformative-change-215683aa80b1.

4 Katie Stubley, personal conversation, September 2024.

Acknowledgments

This book was written by two people but co-generated by a social field: the global community around the Presencing Institute and the u-school for Transformation. The book also emerged from dialogues and collaborations with a wide range of changemakers and innovators across regions. We would like to thank everyone engaged in this deeper work of re-generation and transformation. We would also like to thank our students and partners.

We thank Jeevan Sivasubramaniam and the team at Berrett-Koehler for their amazing support. We thank our three reviewers, Eva Pomeroy, Laura Pastorini, and Vanessa Weyrauch for their detailed feedback, which trans-formed the book.

Huge thanks go to Agathe Peltereau-Villeneuve, Aggie and Martin Kalungu-Banda, Angela Baldini, Anne-Sophie Dubanton, Aya Hijazi, Carrie Hessler-Radelet, Crystal Huang, Deniz Cengiz, Denise Fairchild, Ditri Zandstra, Dorian Baroni, Florentina Bajraktari, Georgiana Ward-Booth, Götz Feeser, Grâce Victoire Gueye, Janice Spadafore, Janine Saponara, Josh Kirschenbaum, John

Heller, John Stubley, Kelvy Bird, Monica Sulecio de Alavarez, Munya Makombe, Rachel Hentsch, and Stefan Day. Your creativity, commitment, and vision of deep transformation carries this community.

Thanks to Cherie Nursalim, Dr. Ben Chan, Frans Sugiarta, Jayce Pei Yu Lee, Julie Arts, Lili Xu, Manish Srivastava, and Shobi Lawalata, for your work and the case stories that inspired this book.

Profound thanks to Adam Yukelson, Antoinette Klatzky, Arawana Hayashi, Becky Buell, Emma Paine, Eva Pomeroy, Katie Stubley, Kenneth Hogg, Laura Pastorini, Maria Daniel Bras, Marian Goodman, and Sebastian Jung for your ongoing work in the field of deep transformation, as well as for sharing your stories in this book and contributing critical edits on several drafts—sometimes under time pressure.

Thanks to Olaf Baldini for your great artwork on the book cover and all the figures, and to Kelvy Bird for creating the first Wheel of Deep Change. Thanks to Kelvy Bird and Arawana Hayashi for pioneering and evolving the social artforms of generative scribing and Social Presencing Theater, which keep inspiring all our work. Many thanks to Patricia Bohl for helping us in so many ways during the final phase of writing this book. Janet Mowery—without your exceptional editing, the book would not be here now.

Thanks to Beth Jandernoa, Dayna Cunningham, Gabriele Lutz, Glennifer Gillespie, Hannah Scharmer, Johan Scharmer, Janice Spadafore, Kerstin and Christian von Plessen, Martin Butzlaff, Melanie Goodchild, and Peter Senge for being supportive friends. Thanks to our families for being there for us and to Dieter and Margret Scharmer for your life's work that inspired this book!

Index

reactive response, 121
reflective dialogue, 108
regeneration, 3, 11–13;
    eco-system awareness,
    42–45; evolving human
    consciousness, 53–54; new
    ways of operating, 163
regenerative agriculture, 32,
    163
regenerative finance, 36
resonance, 114
roadblocks, 144–145
running in circles, 6, 86

Sarma, Sanjay, 127
sat, 91–92
Schein, Ed, 61
Schweickart, Rusty, 142–143
science, rise of, 83
scientific revolutions,
    150–151
seed meditation, 141–142
seeds of the future, 128, 173
self-knowledge, 79–80,
    82–83
Senge, Peter, 113, 128, 143
shifting consciousness, 19–20
silencing, 51
social arts, 168–169
social divide, 16
social field, the, 3–4, 23–24,
    28, 28–29; dialogue, 113,
    115; eco-system leadership,
    96–97; essence of *Theory
    U*, 120–125; nonbinary
    perspective, 95
social media: business
    model of, 48–50;
    destruction narrative, 3;
    disorientation and
    distraction, 16; misinfor-
    mation, 14

social presencing theater,
    128, 168–169
social soil, 3; bending the
    beam back onto ourselves,
    97–98; conditions for
    cultivating, 164–165;
    practices for cultivating, 4,
    6–7, 45–52; quality of,
    51–52, 111; transforma-
    tional shifts, 139–140;
    "Wheel of Deep Change,"
    4–5; *u-school for Transfor-
    mation*, 171
social systems, 3–5; matrix of
    absencing, *49*; relational
    quality, 28–29; systems
    thinking and the iceberg
    model, 24–27; visible and
    invisible parts, 24, *28*
social technologies, 169
soil: analogy with the
    social system, 3–4, 6–7,
    23–24, *28*, 45–46;
    bending the beam back
    onto ourselves, 97–98;
    conditions for cultivating,
    164–165; dialogue,
    110–111; quality of, 51–52;
    seeds of the future, 128;
    social arts, 168–169;
    *u-school for Transforma-
    tion*, 171
source, 89
spheres of change, 5.
    See also "Wheel of Deep
    Change"
spiritual divide, 16
Srivastava, Manish, 102–103,
    121, 122
stillness, 19, 114, 117, 124
stopping, learning how to,
    124–125

stories: destruction versus
    regeneration, 3, 11–13; of
    transformation, 78–79
structural violence, 161–162
Sugiarta, Frans, 65
Supriyanto, Bambang,
    134–136
sustainable agriculture, 32
sustainable development, 25,
    35
sustainable development
    goals (SDGs), 25, 41
sustainable timber, 129–132
systems mirror, 4–5, 31
systems thinking, 24–27,
    125. *See also* social
    systems

Tao (Daoism), 89–90
tax, redistribution of wealth,
    152–153
teaching for testing, 51
technology, 37–39, 48–50;
    business model of Big
    Tech and Big Social
    Media, 48–50; economic
    theory, 149; social
    technologies, 169
terrorism, 62–63, 64
Theory U, 23–24, 28–29;
    essence of, 120–125;
    interview with Francisco
    Varela, 59–60; responding
    to disruption, 86–87;
    source, 89; *Tri Hita
    Karana*, 65–66
thinking together, 110.
    See also dialogue
Thompson, Phil, 126–127
timber trade, sustainability
    of, 129–132
"to be," 91

About the Authors

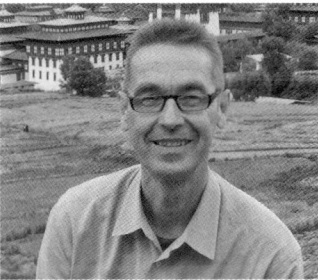

Otto Scharmer is a senior lecturer at MIT and the founding chair of the Presencing Institute. A global thought leader in systems transformation and societal change, he is best known for introducing the concept of "presencing"—learning from the emerging future. Otto is the author of several influential works, including the bestselling *Theory U* and *Presence* (co-authored), as well as *Leading from the Emerging Future* (co-authored), which explores shifting economies from ego-driven to eco-centered paradigms, and *The Essentials of Theory U*, a concise guide to awareness-based systems change.

As a co-founder of the MITx u.lab, a global platform for societal innovation, Otto has reached over 260,000 participants across 194 countries. His work spans collaborations with businesses, governments, UN agencies, and grassroots movements, catalyzing transformative initiatives that advance planetary healing, social regeneration, and deep systems change. For information, visit ottoscharmer.com.

Katrin Kaufer is director of Just Money at the MIT Community Innovators Lab (CoLab) in MIT's Department of Urban Studies and Planning and managing director of the Presencing Institute (presencing.org). Her work and research focuses on leadership, organizational change, and values-based finance as well as on participatory action research. Dr. Kaufer has worked with mid-sized and global companies, non-profit organizations, and international organizations. Her 2013 book, co-authored with Otto Scharmer, is titled *Leading from the Emerging Future*. In 2021 she published *Just Money: Mission-Based Banking and the Future of Finance*. For more information, visit katrinkaeufer.com.

Dear reader,

Thank you for picking up this book and welcome to the worldwide BK community! You're joining a special group of people who have come together to create positive change in their lives, organizations, and communities.

What's BK all about?

Our mission is to connect people and ideas to create a world that works for all.

Why? Our communities, organizations, and lives get bogged down by old paradigms of self-interest, exclusion, hierarchy, and privilege. But we believe that can change. That's why we seek the leading experts on these challenges—and share their actionable ideas with you.

A welcome gift

To help you get started, we'd like to offer you a **free copy** of one of our best-selling ebooks:

bkconnection.com/welcome

When you claim your **free ebook**, you'll also be subscribed to our blog.

Our freshest insights

Access the best new tools and ideas for leaders at all levels on our blog at ideas.bkconnection.com.

Sincerely,

Your friends at Berrett-Koehler